SILENT MUSIC

Other Books by William Johnston

The Mysticism of 'The Cloud of Unknowing'
The Still Point: Reflections on Zen and Christian Mysticism
Christian Zen

Translations
Silence, a novel by Shusaku Endo, translated from the Japanese
The Cloud of Unknowing and The Book of Privy Counselling,
newly edited from the Middle English

SILENT MUSIC

THE SCIENCE OF MEDITATION

Meditation — Consciousness
Healing — and Intimacy

William Johnston

PERENNIAL LIBRARY
Harper & Row, Publishers
New York, Hagerstown, San Francisco, London

SILENT MUSIC: *The Science of Meditation*. Copyright © 1974
by William Johnston. All rights reserved. Printed in the
United States of America. No part of this book may be used
or reproduced in any manner whatsoever without written permission except in the case of brief quotations embodied in
critical articles and reviews. For information address Harper &
Row, Publishers, Inc., 10 East 53d Street, New York, N.Y.
10022. Published simultaneously in Canada by Fitzhenry &
Whiteside Limited, Toronto.

First PERENNIAL LIBRARY edition published 1976.

STANDARD BOOK NUMBER: 06–080386–X

76 77 78 79 80 10 9 8 7 6 5 4 3 2 1

Contents

Preface

It has become a commonplace to say that the human race stands at a
unique point in its turbulent history and that we are faced with a
new age. Talk of travel in outer space and of adventures in inner
space reminds us that things are not what they used to be – that the
old order changes, yielding place to new. Perhaps we really are on
the brink of a brave new world. What kind of world this will be no
one is quite sure. We just feel that something is stirring in the
consciousness of modern man.

Among the many fascinating characteristics of the incipient, new
age is the contemporary longing for dialogue. Already Hindu and
Jew, Christian and Buddhist are coming together in sincerity and
harmony to exchange experiences and to explore common goals.
And as interfaith dialogue gets under way, it finds itself extending a
hand of welcome to an unexpected newcomer on the scene; namely,
the scientist. For now we find a group of serious-minded scientists,
students of consciousness, who express a desire to learn more about
the great religious traditions which have accumulated such wealth
of experiential knowledge about the human mind. These are scholars
who feel that their research will be incomplete unless it takes into
consideration the experiences of the mystic and the discoveries of
the man who meditates.

The religious activity that interests these scientists is not speculative theology but meditation. And this is indeed fortunate. Because
meditation is precisely the area in which the great religions find
themselves most united. I myself have discovered this in discussion
with Buddhists in Japan. We found that dialogue based on theology
and philosophy did not achieve much; but when we talked from
experience we suddenly discovered how closely united we really
were. So it is refreshing to see that the religio-scientific dialogue, like
the inter-religious dialogue, will begin with meditation.

This book, then, is about meditation. Let me say, however, that
the choice of this word has caused me some anguish. I use it in the
widest possible sense to include discursive thinking and reasoning
about ultimate matters as well as what Christians call *contemplation*

and Hindus call *samadhi*[1] and Buddhists call *Zen*. In it I also include mysticism – which, in my opinion, is no more than a very deep form of meditation. It was difficult to find an all-embracing word that would include these disparate things, and it seemed to me that 'meditation' was the best. For me meditation, in the last analysis, is the search for wisdom or the relishing of wisdom when it has been found. As such it is a word and a practice that unites us all. Religionists, scientists, businessmen and statesmen can claim that they are looking for, and feel the need of, wisdom. And how beautiful and attractive this lady is! I am reminded of the Hebrew sage who loved her passionately and sang:

> I loved her and sought her from my youth,
> and I desired to take her for my bride,
> and I became enamoured of her beauty.
> (Wisdom 8:2)

This is the lady who enthralls both scientist and mystic. 'My beloved is the mountains, the solitary wooded valleys, strange islands . . . silent music.'

I sincerely hope that what I here write will be of interest and value to anyone who loves wisdom, whatever his religious affiliations or whatever his lack of them. While I myself am firmly entrenched in the Hebrew-Christian tradition, which I love more deeply than I can say, I have had the inestimable privilege of entering into dialogue with men and women of other faiths and other religious traditions. This has helped me a lot; and I would like this book to be an expression of gratitude to people who have greatly inspired me, even when they did not always share my convictions.

While writing, I have been somewhat fascinated by the word *tao*, meaning *way*. We ordinarily associate this word with oriental thought; and rightly so. But it is also interesting to recall that it is a profoundly biblical word. Its Greek equivalent, ὁδός, is found no less than 880 times in the Septuagint, to say nothing of its frequent use in the Synoptic Gospels, St John and the writings of St Paul. And in many cases its use is figurative, resembling closely that of the Orient. So *way*, like meditation, is a word that brings us together.

---

[1] Explanations of this and other words which may be unfamiliar to the reader are given in the glossary at the end of the book.

There are, I believe, many ways to wisdom. Each religion is a way and within each religion many smaller ways open up. In this book I try to outline some of the ways of meditation such as the repetition of a word or *mantra*, attention to the breathing, the use of the *mandala* and other methods of deepening consciousness. These are ways that are the same, and yet different, according to the faith of the meditator. But I also contend that friendship is a way, as also is purification or healing. And again I believe that the scientist has his way. All these ways influence one another. Knowledge of other ways can help the wanderer to find his own path and it can guide the traveller or pilgrim as he journeys towards wisdom, sometimes in anguish and dismay and temptation.

Dialogue between travellers of the various ways is surely one of the most significant events in our day. As the human race comes together with unprecedented rapidity, anyone with common sense knows that we must get together, form a single family and build the earth. For it is another commonplace that there is no longer any alternative to peace. Can it be that the Lady Wisdom will show us the way to union and harmony?

Finally, let me say that I am greatly indebted to a number of people for the experiences, insights and ideas they shared with me. First, I would like to express my deep gratitude to the Reno Carmelites, and especially to Laureen Grady, who worked with me in the writing of this book. Then I must thank my cousin, Dr Kevin Clearkin, who gave me so many stimulating ideas and so much encouragement – and also his wife, Flora, who looked after our material needs as we talked. Finally, there is Dr Tomio Hirai, of Tokyo University, with whom I spent many pleasant hours sipping green tea while talking about brainwave and biofeedback. His enlightening conversation and his meticulous research have let me see how sincerely the modern scientist searches for wisdom.

Sophia University,
Tokyo.
1974

'My beloved is the mountains, the
solitary wooded valleys, strange
islands . . . silent music'

(St John of the Cross)

PART I

MEDITATION

1. *The meditation movement*

The last decade has witnessed the rise of a great meditation movement which gathers momentum and appeals to men and women in
all walks of life. Zen and Yoga, no longer a monopoly of the East,
have become part of world culture and are practised not only by
Buddhists and Hindus but also by Westerners – many of whom find
in this methodology a way of deepening their traditional faith. Even
more widespread than these, however, is transcendental meditation,
popularly known as TM. Introduced to the West by the Maharishi
Mahesh Yogi, this form of Yoga is now practised by tens of thousands
of people in Europe and America. No doubt one reason for its
popularity and wide appeal is the very simplicity and ease with
which it can be practised by the ordinary person. Though religious
in origin, going back for several millennia, the transcendental
meditation introduced to the West is not attached to any one
religion. Rather is it a means for developing human potential, thus
enabling people to devote themselves with greater totality to the job
on hand or to commit themselves more fully to their vocation.

Transcendental meditation has had its greatest success with
students and young professors, but it is not without impact on the
world of business. For, yes, the world of economics, too, casts an
eye in the direction of meditation. We now hear the interesting news
that business tycoons discover the value of silence and of the quiet
room to which bruised and harassed executives can retire to find
peace and inner security. And here another kind of meditational
exercise is speedily making headway – meditation associated with
biofeedback and the use of machines. This has been called 'electronic
yoga' and I would like to say more about it later. For now, enough to
quote the *New York Times* for 16 April 1972 on 'the biofeedback
revolution that some people say is flowing over the country, creating
a multi-million dollar industry with broad implications for physicians,
government officials, teachers, scientists and businessmen'. I laughed
when I read this because the only class omitted from the list of
interested persons is the clergy. Have they lost their interest in
meditation? Or will they too become part of the business that is fast

becoming part of modern culture and is already entering the curriculum of our schools? Be that as it may, biofeedback machines, advertised as teachers of meditation, are already cheaply available (though admittedly good ones are not cheap) and with them most people can learn in some measure to regulate their internal states of consciousness. No doubt transistorized biofeedback machines will soon be exported in large quantities from Japan and introduced to the hungry West.

Again, meditation in the business world is frequently linked to the numerous mind-control courses that are everywhere springing up. These courses teach deep relaxation and claim to introduce people to profound and subtle layers of psychic life. I had an opportunity to attend one such course in downtown New York. We were taught to take up a comfortable position, relax and 'get our level'; that is to say, to enter into a deeper and healthier level of mind beyond the consciousness concerned with discursive reasoning. For anyone who has practised a little meditation this is not new; but the mind-control course went on to speak, somewhat alarmingly, about thought-projection, about programming oneself and others, about the diagnosis of illness, about psychic healing and all kinds of para-psychological activities. This was more challenging. It was not only a course in the power of positive thinking but also in the development of psychic powers. One aspect of the thing that interested me personally was the emphasis placed on visualization. We were taught to visualize minutely the place in which we could best relax, or the person with whom we wished to communicate telepathically. Visualization, it was claimed, makes this exercise more effective; and this interested me in view of the stress placed on visualization in certain religious traditions of meditation. It is not my intention here to evaluate mind-control. Enough to say that, even if I could not accept everything and if, alas, my telepathic efforts got me nowhere, I had a pleasant four days with a charming group of people. I had been led to think that these courses make their appeal to grim-jawed stockbrokers, red-faced businessmen and hard-nosed politicians; but the one I attended was not like that. In our group the feminine and artistic element predominated. A delightful, if exhausting, time was had by all.

Within Christianity, too, meditation is in vogue. Traditionally, it is true, silent and wordless contemplation was mainly for an élite of monks and nuns; but in recent times the people at large have shown a desire for deeper meditation. One of its popular forms is the famous *Jesus Prayer* which originated in the early Greek Church and was associated with the Hesychast movement. Like transcendental meditation this is practised by the constant repetition of a *mantra* or sacred word, in this case the word 'Jesus'. Not only are the vibrations important, the meaning of the word is also of the greatest significance. Through it one becomes more and more committed to, and identified with, the Jesus whose name is invoked. In some Pentecostal groups, too, a meditational dimension seems to be taking shape. Perhaps people are beginning to feel the need of solitude and silence to complement the communal experience that characterizes this form of shared prayer. Not that contemplation is necessarily absent from group worship. Most people who have taken part in group prayer will have sensed the deep interior silence that sometimes enshrouds the whole gathering as though the Spirit were palpably present. This, I believe, is a type of communal contemplation, a form of meditation that is particularly marked in a community of love. Here it is not only the individual but also the group that relishes an obscure sense of enveloping presence. Such an experience can also be found in Quaker meetings. Indeed this is a dimension of prayer that the Friends have always preserved and now share with others in a spirit of ecumenical generosity.

Again within Christianity there is the arrival of Christian Zen. While it is true that Christianity is still groping experimentally with this form of meditation, things are beginning to happen. Not long ago, a Japanese Zen master in the USA donned the Cistercian habit and led a retreat or *sesshin* for Christian monks, giving them as their *koan* the paradoxical and enigmatic problem, 'What do you mean when you make the sign of the cross?' This was interesting for me because it confirmed my conviction that the crucifix is the great Christian *koan*. Be that as it may, in the coming decade some form of Zen may well develop within Christianity, enriching it with a new and beautiful dimension.

Many more instances of meditation movements could be cited. I mention these few; and it will be noticed that the common factor uniting such disparate things is a tendency to go beyond the emotional and intellectual consciousness to the deeper, more unified, intuitive or mystical consciousness. That is why these forms of meditation have few words. And sometimes they have no words at all. One is simply held in intense silence and unification, only conscious of the breathing or the beating of the heart or an obscure sense of presence. Modern people, it seems, are less attracted by wordy prayer. 'In praying do not heap up empty phrases as the Gentiles do; for they think that they will be heard for their many words' (Matthew 6:7). People are now looking for silence, for depth, for interiority, for what has traditionally been called contemplation. They want something that opens up deeper layers of consciousness, bringing into play the more subtle and mystical faculties of the mind. This is what elsewhere I have called 'vertical meditation' because it spirals down into its own silent depths, to the core of the being. Perhaps it is because this kind of meditative silence is found in the Japanese tea-ceremony, flower arrangement, archery and the rest that these have greatly attracted Western interest in recent times.

No doubt one reason for this boom is the realization that meditation brings interior unity. This is stressed by a medieval English mystic who charmingly speaks of meditation as a 'oneing exercise' because it makes us whole. And the modern denizen of technopolis, torn asunder by the intolerable pressures of the global village and by the total involvement demanded by TV and advertising, finds himself torn in pieces by anguish, guilt and anxiety. And so he longs for unity and strength to cope with future shock. McLuhan said well that man must learn to defend himself against the tyranny of mass media; but he did not say clearly how this can be done. Many people seem to have found that meditation is one answer. Businessmen, psychologists and religionists are beginning to feel that it may indeed be so.

Now, as I have pointed out, a fascinating aspect of this whole meditation boom is that it is by no means confined to the ostensibly or professionally religious. We find ourselves confronted with the paradoxical picture of people meditating night and morning while claiming that they believe in nothing – neither in God nor in Christ nor in Krishna nor in the Buddha. In short, there is abroad a secular or seemingly agnostic brand of mystical meditation that disclaims affiliation with any religion and is totally devoted to the development of human potential. One might ask if twentieth-century man, having secularized art, music, poetry, education and politics, has finally decided to do the job properly and secularize prayer. After all, he needs prayer no less than he needs air and water, so he might as well have it without the burdensome trappings and useless paraphernalia of Christianity, Buddhism or anything else. In short, it might look as if the man of the 1970s begins to opt for prayer without religion.

To the traditional Jew or Christian, educated to look on meditation as a cry to God, this may seem incredible and he may wonder why anyone should take the trouble to meditate if he has no faith. But this radically secular meditation is much less strange to the Japanese who have known of such practice for generations. Zen, which originated in China and was practised there for centuries as a religious exercise, was quickly used in Japan, first by *samurai*, then by suicide pilots, and finally by business tycoons. This is one more example of the eminent practicality of the Japanese, who could adapt an originally religious exercise to waging war, making efficient washing-machines, and curing the common cold. Who but the Japanese could have done such a thing? Yet this is precisely what they did. And today one can see groups of fresh young executives sitting assiduously in Zen temples to expand their consciousness and enhance their devotion to the world of economics. And now the West, which knows a good thing when it sees it, follows suit. What makes yen in Tokyo might make dollars on Wall Street or sterling in Piccadilly. So why not give it a try?

But let me not be cynical. Even as I write I am aware that much of the seemingly agnostic meditation is not agnostic at all. Frequently the self-styled agnostic who meditates is searching for something ultimate. And the person who searches believes, or hopes, that an answer exists somewhere. In this sense he is not agnostic. Many meditators are in quest of truth, wisdom, ultimate values – things they have failed to find within their own religious tradition. It could be plausibly argued that secular meditation has arisen partly because traditional and established religion has ceased to give people, particularly young people, the religious experience for which they are craving. So they look elsewhere. They are tired of dogmas and formulations and words – 'Words, words, words!' said Hamlet. However necessary these formulations may be (and some formulation is, I believe, necessary), they can sometimes erect barriers between man and reality. And contemporary man wants reality; he wants experience; he wants practice; he wants a 'way'. Way or *tao*, the great Eastern word used to describe religious experience, appears frequently in the Old Testament; and Christians were called 'followers of the way', just as their founder called himself the Way.

Anyhow, experience of meditation gives people the sense of being on a way that goes somewhere; and that is what they want.

So the religious dimension is not absent from the meditation movement. To say this, however, intimates that I know the meaning of this enigmatic word 'religious'. Much time and effort and energy have been expended in attempts to say what the word means, and as yet there seems to be little unanimity of opinion. So perhaps I will be pardoned for giving my own definition.

Applied to meditation I would say that this exercise is not religious if one is meditating to improve one's general health or to relieve one's backache or to cure a migraine headache or to enhance one's business acumen. However noble and laudable these objectives, even the most broadminded among us will scarcely call them religious. But if, over and above these things (without necessarily excluding them), one is searching for ultimate truth, for values, for wisdom; if one is pre-occupied with what we now call 'ultimate concern', then one's quest is religious. In a nutshell, what makes meditation religious or non-religious is one's sense of values and one's motivation. These are the all-important elements in the whole business.

In this sense I believe that many of the self-styled agnostic meditators are religiously motivated because they are searching for truth. And sooner or later, if they continue their practice, they will be confronted with ultimate questions of life and death and faith and the Absolute.

It will be perfectly clear by now that everything I have said presents a tremendously stimulating challenge to the traditional religions in their institutional forms. I myself believe that they have a great role to play in directing and promoting and inspiring this meditation movement. For the fact is that the development of human potential is a two-edged sword. It simply means that man will have increased powers either for good or for evil, for love or for hate, for war or for peace. More human potential will enable businessmen to exploit the poor or to build the *noosphere*. It may help politicians to enslave millions or to alleviate distress – to make better bombs or to purify the air we breathe. Everything depends on motivation. It is well known in all the great religions that mystical powers can be used for evil as well as for good; and when they are used for evil, the consequences are very, very evil. That is why the meditation movement is a challenge to the great religions, which are called to give values and motivation. They have to give guidance about what is important in life and about the goals towards which increased human potential should be directed. This, religionless meditation will not do. The role of religions will be to teach their gospel to the new, mystical man now emerging in the *noosphere*. They must save him from the quagmire of illusion and insecurity and mystical evil.

Christians have sometimes asked me about the relevance of TM and biofeedback and mind-control for their faith; and I have answered that whatever develops human potential should also develop Christian faith, provided this faith is alive and nourished by scripture and liturgy. I mean that if human potential is enhanced, then the totality of one's commitment to Christ can also be deepened. Having said this, however, I hasten to add my conviction that the Judaeo-Christian tradition will soon have its own, vital part to play in the evolution of this meditation movement. Part of this role will be the sharing with others of the riches of the Western mystical tradition, just as others have generously shared with the West. In order to do this it will be necessary to revitalize and live this Western mysticism, making it relevant for the men of our day, whether they be students or scientists, businessmen or professors, housewives or labourers. If institutional religion has somehow failed those in search of meditation, this is partly because it has been unable to keep pace with the sudden evolutionary leap in consciousness that has characterized the last decade. We are now faced with a new man, a more mystical man, and it is on the mystical dimension of religion that we must fix our attention.

explains the emphasis
of the movement in
consciousness and
calls on us to share
the riches of Western
Mysticism

empt to develop human
potential

2. *The new science*

Perhaps the most intriguing aspect of the meditation movement is not the interest of students, professors and businessmen, but that of the scientists. For the scientists are the prophets of our day; when they praise a commodity the populace hastens to buy. But why this scientific interest?

For one thing it stems from a growing preoccupation with 'altered states of consciousness'. At the beginning of the century William James shrewdly observed in a famous sentence that our normal waking consciousness is but one special type of consciousness, while around it, parted from it by the flimsiest screens, there lie potential forms of consciousness entirely different. In other words, within the human mind are many, many worlds that are uncharted and unknown. Now psychologists become increasingly interested in these worlds; they become aware of the almost infinite possibilities for exploration in the field of human consciousness. It would seem that all the popular talk about exploratory trips in inner space is not just science fiction. Inner space is going to be quite as enthralling as outer space. LSD, mescalin and suchlike drugs (whatever may be said about their abuse) do reveal a new environment, a new world, another dimension of reality; and the psychophysiology of awareness promises to be one of the most exciting adventures of our exciting age. In short, we find ourselves at the threshold of a new science. This is the science of consciousness, of mind-expansion, of enhanced awareness.

This new science has received a boost from a series of conferences held at Council Grove in Kansas over the past few years and attended by psychiatrists, physicists, theologians, physicians, mathematicians, psychologists and engineers, from Denmark, Iceland, India, Japan, Germany, Canada, France, Chile and England. For the first session, called the 'Interdisciplinary Conference on the Voluntary Control of Internal States of Consciousness', the invitation to the participants contained the following paragraph:

The calling of a conference on states which have been variously termed altered states of consciousness, expanded consciousness, or states of internal awareness, is precipitated by the need for research in the domain of consciousness itself. We have reached a point in history at which the exploration of 'internal states' has become not only a legitimate, but also a high-priority business of science. In addition, many people are conducting their own explorations in consciousness with unknown chemicals in psycho-actively-unknown dosages in an attempt to enhance life or escape from it. This can be a dangerous route to 'freedom'. The Conference Committee feels that at this moment it is especially important for stabilizing forces to be brought to bear that link what is useful from the past with the present and the future, uniting in some degree the existential wisdom and psychology of the East and the different psychological insights of the West.

(Green (1))

The above reminds me of Teilhard's contention that we now stand at a unique point in human history, when the time is ripe for the development of a science of man; it also reveals the great contemporary interest in consciousness. Today even the man in the street (about whom we now hear so little) gets interested in recording his dreams and daydreams, while the scientist turns his attention not only to dreams but also to hypnotic trance, drug experience, and all that goes by the name of altered states of consciousness. A few serious psychologists begin to say that in the process of evolution man's brain and nervous system are developing a psychological and physiological need for these altered states – a need for a new kind of 'high' that has not been found through drugs, alcohol and sex.

Now obviously anyone interested in states of consciousness will enjoy something of a field-day when he comes to meditation, particularly to the meditation of the mystics who, centuries ago, experienced states that the psychologist is only now beginning to envisage. All meditation, once it gets deep, produces changes in the electrical activity of the brain, bringing the conscious and unconscious mind into closer proximity. The conscious mind impinges, so to speak, on the unconscious and is thus opened to receive messages and enlightenment from the dark and subliminal depths of one's being in a process that is analogous to, but different from, dreaming. 'Zen is the prayer of the unconscious', remarked a bright student of mine. I would prefer to say that it is the prayer of the unconscious made conscious or becoming conscious. But be that as it may, the traditional metaphors for describing contemplative prayer – about spiritual sleep and so on – indicate the working of new levels of consciousness in the mystical depths of the mind, and cannot fail to attract the attention of the researcher in inner space.

Yet it is only in recent years that the scientist has begun to take notice of this profound human adventure that we call meditation. Asserting that scientific knowledge of this meditative realm of psychic life is totally inadequate, Dr Charles Tart of the University of California at Davis pleads for more research in this field:

> It seems likely that research in this area has been too long delayed through a combination of ignorance and prejudice. Scientists in general simply have not known anything about the rich tradition of meditation, and the intimate connection of meditation practices with religion has further removed it from the area of 'acceptable' topics of study . . . Although prediction is premature, the potential contributions of the experimental study of meditation to such diverse areas as perceptual vigilance, psychotherapy, and creativity, in both a theoretical and practical sense, warrant a greatly expanded research effort.   (Tart, p. 176)

Since the above was written in 1964, considerable progress has been made. Yet it can still be said that, while altered states have been around for millennia, the science that investigates them is still in its infancy. Most researchers gladly admit to their appalling ignorance of the human mind. Even vocabulary-wise we are at a loss. In Sanskrit there are more than twenty words for what we blandly call 'mind'. But scientific jargon is being born. Now, not only ASC for *altered states of consciousness*, but also MSC for *meditation states of consciousness*, and HSC for *higher states of consciousness* and EIA for *enhanced internal awareness*. Personally I am glad and happy about the distinction between altered states of consciousness and meditation states of consciousness because I believe that the states arrived at through meditation are not 'altered' in the sense of being bizarre or abnormal. Rather are they the most normal of states – states that every man should pass through to fulfil his great vocation of hominization or becoming a man.

So we have a new science. And it is interesting to see that for a number of scientists the study of meditation states of consciousness *personal experience is essential*

is not just academic. It is also practical. I personally have met a number of scientists who themselves practise meditation and experience to some extent the states of consciousness that are the object of their research. They say they would feel unqualified to talk about these states without some degree of personal experience.

After the fourth meeting at Council Grove, one of the participants described the proceedings in a paper entitled 'Towards a Science Concerned with Ultimates'. The very title surprised me. Though it is true that Aristotle, wise old Greek, was an astronomer and a physicist and a historian who jumped the traces and entered the field of ultimates which he called metaphysics, I did not expect modern scientists to follow his example. For Aristotle metaphysics was the science of causes and the greatest science (the so-called 'first philosophy') was the science of ultimate causes or of *the* ultimate cause. That was how he got involved with the Prime Mover and 'the thought that thinks itself'. And do modern scientists now follow his example? Are they, too, going to look for a Prime Mover? If so, they would follow the example of Teilhard, whose science led him to the conclusion that there must be an Omega, a Prime Mover ahead, the point of convergence of the evolutionary process. Or Jung, who at the end of his life declared that he had always seen something permanent beneath the eternal flux. Or Einstein, who said that God does not play dice with the universe. These are big names. They risked their reputation and jeopardized their credibility by talking like this. But things have moved since they lived and thought; and now we find scientists following in their footsteps, 'extrapolating' in the same way, asking about ultimates and even about religion. The fourth Council Grove meeting, called for the study of transcendental things, ended with a declaration which is both novel and profound:

> Our group decided he [the scientist] should admit he doesn't know anything.
> Our group thought he should study transcendental things in a questioning way.
> A scientist is a human being, and should deal with personal matters in a human way.
> He should read the 'scientific journals' [i.e. great spiritual systems] of other cultures. The science of consciousness has already been written.

Most science of consciousness material is related to personal escape.

But Mohammed lived in society.

These inner forces are very powerful. Beware the great 'dangers that exist when work like this is done, especially by large numbers of people, without the high values and lifelong discipline of the great ancient systems.

The role of science is testing out old ideas.

What makes old ideas new is taking them seriously.   (Weide, p. 84)

As a statement from scientists this has a fresh and humble ring. I think it was Plato or Socrates who said that the first step towards wisdom is the acknowledgement of one's own ignorance; and these scientists have done just that. And then the feeling that they really must read the great spiritual systems with their 'scientific journals'. By this I suppose they mean that the researcher in consciousness must get to work and read the Upanishads, the Sutras, the Bible, the fathers of the Church, St Teresa of Avila, *The Cloud of Unknowing*, the Koran, and all the rest. Pretty enthralling reading for the scientist indeed. Again, profound is their realization that powerful forces are unleashed with consequent dangers. Anyone with the slightest experience of meditation knows about the uprising of the unconscious and the possible resultant turmoil, to say nothing of the increased psychic power that meditation brings. All this could have the greatest social consequences if meditation becomes widespread. Yes, the high values, the lifelong discipline and the wisdom of the great spiritual systems are not to be overlooked. When you build a tower you'd better sit down and count the cost.

The only statement in the above declaration that makes me hesitate is that which asserts that the science of consciousness has already been written. That it has partly been written I do not doubt. But is it finished? Has the curtain come down? I prefer to believe that it has a pretty bright future and that there is another act. More will be experienced; more will be written; more facts will come to light. Is it not possible that we will continue to have mystics of the calibre of Paul or the Buddha or Mohammed or Augustine or Ramakrishna? Why not? There is a Buddhist saying that the disciple who does not go beyond his master is not worthy of his master. And did not Jesus say, 'He who believes in me will also do the works that I do; *and greater works than these will he do*, because I go to the Father' (John

14:12)? Going to the Father, he would send the Spirit to teach his disciples all things.

But let me not quibble over details. The significant thing about all this is that some leading scientists are at last stretching out a friendly hand of dialogue towards religion. And I do hope that this time the religionists will not let them down. Surely this dialogue is long overdue. In the past two centuries these two great forces have moved successively from friendship to enmity and on to peaceful co-existence. What progress for humanity if once again they could get really reconciled and go about the work of building the earth!

Some time ago, I and my colleagues invited a number of friends, Buddhist and Christian and scientist, to our place in Tokyo to discuss the inroads of science into meditation and religion. This topic is particularly relevant in Tokyo where a couple of universities (Komazawa and Tokyo University) are sponsoring rather extensive research on the psychophysiology of meditation, measuring the activity of the brain, plotting its course and tabulating the results. It seemed like a good idea to exchange views on this whole thing; and we did so over a *suki-yaki* dinner with beer and then coffee. I must confess that a few of the guests reacted negatively; they felt that the inner life was just too sacred for this kind of experimentation. Meditation in the laboratory, like sex in the laboratory, was the dehumanization of something sacred. Moreover they agreed with à Kempis that the grace of devotion should be concealed by humility and so they took a dim view of people who would get themselves wired up to machines, thus manifesting their *samadhi* to the world. But this was not the opinion of the majority. Most of the participants felt that the time had come for dialogue – that we should stop talking about the *limits* of science and talk instead about the *contribution* of science to meditation and religion. It was even suggested that religion had better have dialogue with science or run the risk of going out of business.

While I myself was all in favour of dialogue with science, I could sympathize with those who reacted negatively to experiments in the neurophysiology of meditation. After all, it would be pretty sad if churches and meditation halls were turned into laboratories for experimentation on the human mind. Shades indeed of the brave new world! But, on the other hand, this need not be so; and such an idea is far from the minds of the scientists I have met. What they want to do is to measure the physiological repercussions of the sacred

practice of meditation, always respecting the area of mystery which
science cannot enter and which is the special field of the religionist
and the mystical theologian. Seeing the trepidation with which their
scientific effort is greeted by some religious people, I am reminded
of the storm over depth psychology and psychoanalysis. Seventy or
eighty years ago psychology was 'the new science'. Religion generally
feared and opposed it. This was a pity since religious influence might
have served and helped direct a science that was to make a strong
impact on society. Only after several decades did religious people
awaken to the immense significance of psychology and the incalculable value of its findings for religion and for meditation. Now at last
religious psychology is an indispensable part of theology and, as is
well known, it exercised considerable influence on Vatican II. Will
the same hold true for neurophysiology? Some of our guests seemed
to think so.

Coming to practicalities, we finally felt that the psychologist, the
psychiatrist, the neurologist and the rest have a lot to offer to the
meditators and their directors. For one thing there is the fact that
meditators sometimes get sick. 'Zen attracts sick people!' exclaimed
one psychologist who practises Zen. And I believe that the same can
be said of most forms of silent meditation. Not infrequently con-
sultation with a doctor is necessary before even starting on the
meditational journey; and later to distinguish between enlightenment
and sickness, between the joy of *satori* and the manic phase of a
manic-depressive personality. But apart from this, science is
investigating the ideal external conditions for meditation – the place,
the lighting, the bodily posture, the diet, the sleep. All this is not
without value and it is interesting to see how often scientific research
confirms ancient religious traditions about diet and posture. Though
it is also true that science sometimes will do away with ancient
taboos.

More important than this, however, are the discoveries now being
made in the field of consciousness itself. Not long ago people (both
wise and not so wise) tended to lump together mysticism, hypnosis,
schizophrenic experience, drug experience and other altered states,
as though they were all variations of a single theme. And this was
not so terribly foolish because to distinguish these states scientifically
is not easy. Yet now, thanks to rigorous laboratory experiments, it
becomes possible to distinguish between the consciousness of Zen
and that of Yoga; it is possible to demonstrate from the brainwaves

that hypnosis is not the same as *samadhi* or the prayer of quiet. Even within Zen, fine research is showing a difference between the *Rinzai* and *Soto* consciousness. All this will help masters and directors who, after all, should know as much as possible about the kind of consciousness they wish to produce and the kind they wish to reject.

Granted, then, that there should be dialogue between religion and science on the subject of meditation, let me say a word on the process of *dialogue*, about which a whole philosophy is already in the making.

Quite clearly the aim of dialogue is not to prove that I am right and you are wrong; nor is its aim to win you to my way of thinking. In dialogue one *explains* with courage and clarity and without pretence, while the other *listens* as sympathetically as possible. Neither party need *compromise* on basic issues, but both *share*. A good example is the dialogue between Zen and Christianity in which I have had the privilege of taking part. As a result of this dialogue no Christian has become a Buddhist nor has any Buddhist become a Christian; but we have shared and greatly profited from our meetings. And in the same way, as the religio-scientific dialogue comes into its own, each party must retain its own identity. Religion must remain religious and science must remain scientific. Only then will there be any real dialogue, any real sharing, any real growth.

Now to do this properly it seems to me that mysticism must be recognized as an autonomous and unique science with psychological, physiological and neurological dimensions – but with a deeply religious core that is not determined by other disciplines. This is frequently recognized by scientists, as for example by one distinguished professor of Tokyo University who explained to me that he was not studying consciousness itself but only the neurophysiological basis of consciousness. And this, he said, is a different thing. It is one thing to study the psychological and physiological repercussions of a human activity and it is quite another to study the activity itself. For the fact is (and this professor grasped it intuitively) that there is something in man that escapes all attempts at delineation and can never be measured by human methodology. For example, psychology and neurology cannot tell us who is a good man. In the eschatological age, people will stand before the Master and say, 'Lord, we worked miracles in your name. We cast out devils. We produced alpha waves; we altered our consciousness; we expanded our minds like elastic.' And the Master may well answer, 'Amen, I say to you, I know you not.' For all these exterior criteria and measurements, however valuable, don't get to the heart of the matter; they don't penetrate to the deepest caverns of motivation and love. That these deep caverns are not known to others nor even to ourselves is one of the great points stressed in the leading religious traditions and more especially in the gospel. Here again we read that the just will be surprised to hear themselves called just. They'll raise their eyes in astonishment and say, 'Lord, when did we see thee hungry and feed thee . . . ?' (Matthew 25:37) And yes, by human reckoning it was pretty reasonable that the men who slaved all day in the vineyard should get more pay than the fellows who turned up later. But that is not the way things worked. There is an element of mystery here. And in the same way we can never equate the attainment of wisdom or the actualization of one's Buddha nature or union with God with any empirical experience that can be measured by man or machine or the most delicate computer.

Most scientists will, I believe, accept this; but the problem with science is that it does not remain pure science for long. It quickly becomes technology and then there arises the danger of glorifying technique at the expense of human values. We have seen this in other areas. At one time there was a great cult of technique for getting the maximum pleasure out of sex. A whole literature appeared on the art of sexual intercourse, complete with up-to-date translations of the *Kama Sutra* and the yoga of sex and all the rest. And then some leading psychiatrists began to protest that all the emphasis on technique destroyed something that was primarily an expression of love. Next an attempt was made to turn friendship into a technique of how to win friends and influence people with all the tricks of the trade. But this, too, had a hollow ring. And this is very relevant when we come to practise meditation or mysticism. Here also is a way of love – it is the deepest love for the Lady Wisdom who cries out in the streets. Let us not overwhelm it with technique. One shudders to think of the advertisements: '*Satori* in one week or money back.'

Meditation in the Judaeo-Christian tradition is nothing less than a love affair between two free agents. That is why it finally cannot be tied down and analysed in terms of alpha and beta and delta. A strange love affair this, a strange kind of intercourse, where the beloved is 'the mountains, the solitary wooded valleys, strange islands . . . silent music'. 'O that his left hand were under my head, and that his right hand embraced me!' (Song of Solomon 2:6) This aspect of the loving relationship is eminently clear in the Bible where Yahweh is the bridegroom and the people are the bride – sometimes the faithful wife, often the wanton harlot. In the writings of the Church fathers frequently it is the human person who is the bride, while Christ is bridegroom.

This notion of the love affair is less evident in Buddhism, where wisdom is not personal. Yet even here I have sometimes found a hint of something similar. I was impressed when a Buddhist monk once remarked to me that *samadhi* is the bodhisattva's wife, and he said that this was reiterated in the early sutras. He was speaking in the context of celibacy, but his remark indicates that the notion of the loving relationship can be close to the heart of the Buddhist meditational ideal. Indeed, the Buddhist, the Jew and the Christian are lovers, foolishly in love with wisdom. That is why they can understand one another well. For the Buddhist, this wisdom is the exquisitely beautiful *prajna*. For the Jew, it is the Torah, and the Lady Wisdom who cries out in the street. For the Christian, wisdom is a person, Jesus Christ, since he is, in the words of Paul, 'the power of God and the wisdom of God' (1 Corinthians 1:24).

Here is the real contribution that religion can make through dialogue to a scientific or secular meditation. It can save it from a mechanistic end by adding the distinctively human dimension. We all know that the great tragedy of the brave new world and other scientific paradises is precisely that they are inhuman. One role of religion is to humanize and to introduce love.

Let me conclude, then, with the suggestion that we take an interdisciplinary approach to the vast and complex field of religious meditation. Broadly, I would divide the study of meditation into two autonomous sciences, one secular and the other sacred. The secular science, containing many subdivisions, would study the psychological, physiological, neurological dimensions of consciousness, leaving the theologian to speak (or, perhaps we should say, stammer) about the area of mystery and faith and grace that lies beyond the cloud of unknowing. Then by dialogue between these two disciplines we may progress into the future.

3. *Brainwave and biofeedback*

The science of consciousness suffers somewhat from its popularizers. Having had the opportunity to speak with specialists both in Tokyo and the US, I have been amazed at the difference between their attitude and that of the popular magazines. These latter talk blithely about alpha, biofeedback machines and the entrance into blissful states. The researchers, on the other hand, keep saying that they know almost nothing about the human brain and even less about the human mind. Faced with new discoveries in the area of consciousness, they are (as one researcher put it to me) like Columbus when he set foot on a new continent. Or they are 'like stout Cortez, when with eagle eyes he stared at the Pacific', confronted with uncharted territory, with unexplored continents, with undreamt-of universes. Moreover they are not a little alarmed by popularization that may bring their work into disrepute.

Having said all this, let me hasten to add that it is not my intention to write here with scientific rigour, and in this sense I am among the popularizers. Having become aware of the great complexities of the matter, I simply intend to summarize aspects of recent scientific research with a view to discussing their implications for religious meditation. For what I say about this scientific study I am greatly indebted to Dr Tomio Hirai of Tokyo University with whom I have had the privilege of doing some work, and also to other specialists in the US who were generous to me with their time, with their learning and with their publications.

Research in the field of consciousness owes a great debt to the German scientist, Hans Berger, who in the 1920s discovered brainwaves and their relation to varying states of consciousness. Thanks to his pioneering work we now know that the brain emits faint electrical impulses which can be measured in microvolts by an electroencephalograph or EEG. Concretely, in their work of experimentation the researchers paste electrodes on the scalp of the subjects to be tested and hook them up to the EEG, which contains an amplifier. This amplifies the tiny electrical potentials as much as ten million times. Then the brainwaves or brain rhythms are traced with automatic ink pens on a revolving scroll. Since there are many types of brainwave, the EEG may be equipped to filter out the particular brainwave one wishes to record.

There are four principal brainwaves, measured according to frequency or speed of impulse and amplitude or voltage strength of the impulse. Researchers ask subjects being tested to describe their internal states while they are producing certain brainwaves; and in this way they are finding that certain internal psychological states of the mind are consistently associated with a corresponding activity of the brain.

The four principal brainwaves are as follows:

Beta is the most common in our waking hours. Beta consciousness, measuring 13 or more cycles per second, is associated with focused attention and the active thinking of a mind turned towards the outside world. In this rhythm the highest degree of cortical excitability is manifested. The reader of these pages is now presumably producing a good deal of beta.

Alpha is more restful. In it the frequency is lowered to 8–12 cycles per second and the internal state is described as one of 'relaxed awareness' with a move towards interiority or what are called 'internally focused states'. Though about 10 per cent of the population of the US are non-alpha-producers, most people produce alpha when they close their eyes and relax. But to continue in alpha consciousness steadily with open eyes is not easy. Indeed it can rarely be done without ascetical training and is one of the characteristics of adepts in Zen. Alpha can be of high or low amplitude according to the production of microvolts by the brain. High-amplitude alpha indicates that the subject is in a rather deep state of concentration; this rhythm is associated with more advanced meditation and with mysticism.

Theta (4–7 cycles per second) is associated with drowsiness. It is the rhythm that appears when one slips towards unconsciousness or towards sleep, and it is often accompanied by dream-like hypnagogic imagery.

Delta (0–4 cycles per second) is the rhythm found in deep sleep.

Perhaps the brainwaves can be understood more easily by glancing at the following two diagrams:

Normally Unconscious		Normally Conscious	
Delta	Theta	Alpha	Beta
1 4	8	13	26

Hertz (cycles per second)

Major frequency bands
in the electroencephalographic (EEG) second

(By kind permission of Dr Elmer Green)

イ 興奮時

図 3

ロ 安静時

ハ 入眠時

ニ 中等度の睡眠（紡錘波期）

ホ 深睡眠

(By kind permission of Dr Tomio Hirai)

EEG graph paper showing the different brainwaves. The
Japanese characters on the left describe the brainwaves. From
top to bottom: excited state (beta); restful state (alpha); drowsy
state (irregular theta); moderate sleep (spindle waves and delta);
deep sleep (delta).

After the discovery of brainwaves a further advance was made by the discovery of biofeedback. This is a technique for human self-monitoring in which a person is made conscious of his brainwaves while at the same time reflecting on his internal state of mind. In other words, it is a mechanical device for presenting information externally about what is happening internally. Our state of consciousness is, so to speak, projected outside so that we can look at it objectively. Concretely, this is done by equipping the EEG with instruments which by sound (the sound of a beep, for example) or by the flashing of a light tell the subject that he is now producing alpha or theta or whatever it may be. By listening for the beep and associating it with certain internal states, he can gradually train himself to enter internal states of consciousness previously only accessible to very gifted people or to drug-users or to mystics. But again one must be cautious. The mechanism of these machines is incredibly delicate. Good biofeedback machines, say the researchers, are not easily come by and they cost money. An inferior machine may cause absurdities. It may make twitching of the scalp sound like alpha, thus raising false hopes in the unfortunate practitioner.

Biofeedback is still in the early stages. But it may well point to a new form of mind-control and to new horizons in education. Its possibilities are enormous.

The rhythm that has evoked most interest in recent times is alpha; and it is already surrounded by myth, with talk of alphatology, alphagenesis, and so on. It seems moreover that a particular personality type tends to be an 'alpha-producer' more or less naturally. Let me quote some descriptions of the alpha-producer from a leading researcher in the field. Dr Joseph Kamiya of the Langley Porter Institute in San Francisco asks subjects to describe their interior dispositions during the various brain rhythms, and this is what he says:

Tentatively, I have found that there are certain kinds of individuals that do much better at learning how to control alpha, especially learning to increase alpha; and these individuals so far seem to be those who have had some interest in and practice of what I shall loosely call 'meditation'. It doesn't necessarily have to be of the Zen or Yoga school or any other formal school of meditation. If the individual has a long history of introspection on his own, he seems to be especially good at enhancing the alpha rhythm. Also he is likely to be an individual who uses words like *images*, *dreams*, *wants*, and *feelings*. I have come to the conclusion that there are a large number of people who really don't know exactly what you are talking about when you talk about images and feelings. To such people the words describe something some-body else might have; but these people do not seem to have any degree of sensitivity to such things themselves. These people do not do well in my experiments, they do not gain a high degree of control over their alpha rhythms.   (Tart, p. 514)

So Dr Kamiya tentatively concludes that people who meditate enter easily into alpha. And probably the converse is also true: the alpha-producers veer towards meditation and the contemplative life. This thesis is confirmed by experiments on Zen in Tokyo University and on Transcendental Meditation in Harvard. In both cases it was found that the meditators moved quickly into alpha and the experienced meditators into high-amplitude alpha, thus showing that the frequency of the rhythms is lowered as one enters deeply into meditation. Another interesting point is the way of suppressing alpha, technically known as 'alpha blocking'. Here again is Dr Kamiya:

I would often hear that visual imagery was the answer [to the problem of how to suppress alpha], that all they would have to do was to conjure up an image of a person's face, hold it, and look at it very *carefully*, so much so that they could actually see the features of the person's face.   (Tart, p. 510)

From this it is clear that focused awareness blocks alpha. And blocking is also caused by any kind of agitation or excitement.

While in the US I had an opportunity to visit Langley Porter to see the equipment and to meet some interesting people. As the researchers kindly told me about their tests with *roshi* and *swami* and various *gurus* from the East, I asked in a flash of Irish chauvinism why they didn't test some Christian monks. They replied that they did. They tested some Catholic clergymen. But whereas the yogis and masters sat silently in majestic splendour registering exquisite and impeccable alpha, the clergymen read the Bible, sang hymns, wandered around the room and fouled up the machines. On hearing this, I blushed for the Holy Roman Church.

Undismayed, however, I reflected that they may have asked the wrong people, and I suggested that they experiment with Cistercian or Carthusian monks who have a long tradition of silent and image-less meditation.

Shortly after this I had occasion to visit a convent in north California where contemplative men and women had gathered for some days of silence and recollection. So I made use of the oppor-tunity to invite a researcher to come along with a portable biofeed-back machine and do some Christian contemplative experimentation. The contemplatives were very cooperative in getting wired up; and, as I had expected, all the persons tested produced high-amplitude alpha. This was more heartening; and although this experimentation could not be carried out with the scientific rigour of the laboratory, it would seem to confirm Dr Kamiya's insight that not only Zen and Yoga but any form of contemplation brings into play the lower-frequency brainwaves.

Seeing this, one can understand why the old spiritual masters discouraged conceptualization and discursive thinking in time of contemplation. What they were discouraging was the focused awareness or the superficial visualization which characterizes conceptual thought. This, as Dr Kamiya has shown, blocks alpha and brings one into beta, thus destroying the conditions most favourable to contemplative experience. Put in scientific terms, what the spiritual masters wanted was to bring their disciples into an alpha state and keep them there, intuitively realizing the value of this neurological conditioning.

Let me remark here, however, that while all contemplation is probably alpha, not all alpha is contemplation. This is important. Contemplation is much more than a certain kind of brainwave; and there is a whole area of motivation, of faith, of grace and the rest which transcends scientific experimentation to enter the cloud of unknowing. About this dimension of mystery more will be said; so let me pass on to some reflections about experiments performed in Tokyo.

Tokyo is a pretty good place for the psychophysiological study of meditation, since here one has sensitive equipment, able scientists and cooperative Zen masters. What more could be desired? Let me, then, say a word about the research on Zen consciousness made by Dr Tomio Hirai of the University of Tokyo.

The most basic experiment (and one that confirms the findings of Dr Kamiya) was done with practitioners of Zen – some with decades of experience, others with little experience, and some practising Zen for the first time. Electrodes were pasted to the frontal, parietal and occipital areas of the brain and hooked to the EEG. (I might add that, besides the brain rhythms, the pulse-rate, respiration, muscle relaxation and skin resistance were also tested – but this need not detain us here.) Results showed that whereas those with no experience of Zen registered beta with bursts of alpha when the eyes were closed, the Zen masters almost immediately entered alpha, even though their eyes were open. This alpha, beginning at the frontal and moving to the parietal and occipital areas of the brain, increased in amplitude and decreased in frequency as the meditation progressed. In some cases it developed into rhythmical theta trains. After the meditation, alpha waves continued for some time.

Furthermore, it was observed that those disciples selected by the master as proficient in Zen conformed most closely to this pattern; and there was a clear correlation between the EEG graph and the number of years spent in *zazen*, which seems to confirm the correlation between brainwaves and internal psychological states. All agree that one of the most interesting aspects of this experiment is the long theta trains which frequently appear after thirty or forty minutes of meditation in the case of proficients. This seems to be a phenomenon the full significance of which is not yet fully understood. I shall return to it later.

A second experiment is called by Dr Hirai 'the click experiment'. The EEG shows that if a person in alpha hears a click or noise, the jolt will cause alpha blocking and bring him back to beta. But if the click is constantly repeated, the person may get accustomed to it and simply cease to react. Now one might expect that proficients in Zen would be so absorbed in their practice as not to hear the click at all or that they would habituate immediately. But the contrary is true. The proficient in Zen never habituates. The EEG shows that his reaction to the click is exactly the same each time he hears it. The extremely brief alpha blocking continues for a fraction of a second each time. This says something important about the Zen consciousness. It shows that the master always hears and sees with the same freshness as if he were hearing or seeing for the first time. To me this is beautiful and fascinating. Here we have a consciousness like that of the natural child, a consciousness filled with wonder and never losing its amazement at the beauty of the sunrise and the falling of the peach blossom. 'Unless you ... become like children ...' (Matthew 18:2).[1]

Another interesting experiment of Dr Hirai is what he calls 'name-calling'. When the subject, all wired-up, enters into Zen meditation, Dr Hirai or one of his colleagues calls out a name and watches for the repercussions on the EEG. In all he has 131 names – the name of the Zen master himself, of his wife and children, the names of Nixon, Cleopatra, Stalin, Marilyn Monroe, famous Japanese movie stars, TV personalities, and whatnot. The person inexperienced in Zen will react very differently according to the name called. The name of his wife or loved ones may cause considerable EEG vibrations whereas the name of Stalin may arouse very little reaction. But in the case of experienced and enlightened Zen masters the reaction to every name called is *exactly the same*. Whether it be Nixon or his wife, the calling of the name causes an infinitesimally small blocking, followed by a return to deep alpha. From this Dr Hirai concludes that the Zen master does not react at all to the *content* of the word called but only to the sound impinging on his ears.

When I told this to some of my friends they expressed a certain amount of dismay. How cold and unfeeling! After all, they said, a man of flesh and blood should react differently to his wife than to Stalin or Cleopatra. Does this man love at all or is he indifferent to human affection? Yet I myself believe that the matter is not quite so simple. It is not, I believe, that the Zen master loves no one, but rather that he is not clinging to anyone or to anything. He is deep in a state of detachment or non-attachment to self-interest; he is in a state of pure beholding which is not only compatible with, but necessary for, the highest love. I came to this conclusion while reading a passage from *The Cloud of Unknowing* which is strikingly parallel. The medieval English author of this work was educated in an asceticism of detachment which valued non-clinging and freedom from self-interest as a path to love. And so he says that in the time of contemplation the contemplative has an equal love for everyone:

But in the contemplative work itself, he does not distinguish

[1] 'I believe the Adult's function in the religious experience is to block out the Parent in order that the Natural Child may reawaken to its own worth and beauty as a part of God's creation.' Thomas Harris in *I'm OK – You're OK* (Harper & Row, New York, 1969), p. 234.

between friend and enemy, brother and stranger. I do not mean, however, that he will cease to feel a spontaneous affection towards a few others who are especially close to him. Of course, he will and frequently, too. This is perfectly natural and legitimate for many reasons known only to love. You will remember that Christ himself had a special love for John and Mary and Peter. The point I am making is that during the work of contemplation everyone is equally dear to him since it is God alone who stirs him to love. He loves all men plainly and nakedly for God; and he loves them as he loves himself.   (Johnston (1), ch. 25)

From the above one can see the similarity between the Zen consciousness and the Christian contemplative consciousness. In either case the names of Cleopatra, Stalin, Nixon and the meditator's wife will cause the same EEG reaction *during the work of contemplation*. Nor is this cold and unfeeling; because 'the warmth of his love reaches out to them all, friends, enemy, stranger and kin alike. If there is any partiality at all, it is more likely to be towards his enemy than towards his friend' (Johnston (1), ch. 25). In this point, as in so many others, the English author of *The Cloud* displays characteristically admirable poise and balance.

But let me now just mention briefly some more conclusions arising from the work of Dr Hirai and others in this field.

First of all, no one can now say that Zen and mysticism are nothing but forms of self-hypnosis. The fact is that the person in hypnotic trance does not necessarily enter into protracted alpha at all. His brain rhythms are more or less like those of any waking, working person. Again, it cannot be said that Zen is just a form of light sleep. Needless to say, the Zen practitioner, like any meditator, might doze off from time to time. But if he does, there is a change in the EEG.

Another interesting conclusion (to which I have made reference in the previous chapter) is the scientific distinction that can now be made between the Zen consciousness and the Yoga consciousness. To the superficial observer these two practices are exactly alike. Both are silent, supraconceptual, unified, imageless, wordless, beyond thought. Moreover in both the meditator produces high-amplitude alpha rhythms. But there the resemblance ends. EEG experiments have shown that if you make a noise, the Zen meditator hears it; if you flash a light, he sees it; if you stick a pin in him, he feels it. This is because his meditation is very much geared to the here and now,

Electrodes pasted to the scalp leading to the selector box which is attached to the EEG.

Kinhin or walking Zen.

See monk in the background wearing gas-mask leading to a gas-bag. This device is designed to measure the output of carbon dioxide.

Electrodes pasted to detect the activity of the various regions of the brain.

to a total presence to reality. In this sense, Zen is extremely incarnational. On the other hand, when the yogi enters into very deep meditation, he hears nothing, sees nothing and feels nothing. So much so that one researcher writes that 'the control of attention achieved by the subject is so intense that neither flashing light, sounding gongs, vibration or the touch of hot glass test-tubes could disrupt the state of concentration and cause alpha-blocking' (Green (3), p. 14).

It will now be clear that for the study of meditation probably the most significant rhythms are alpha and theta.

Fascinating research on alpha-theta trains has been done by Dr Elmer Green at the Menninger Foundation in Kansas. Dr Green associates the alpha-theta train with what he calls 'reverie', a drowsy state found when the mind moves towards sleep or unconsciousness and characterized by the presence of hypnagogic, dream-like imagery (Green (2)). His subjects assert that this imagery is more vivid than that of dreams in that it is much more realistic. 'What were these images like? They were different for each individual of course, yet they shared certain characteristics. They were dreamlike rather than dream, hypnagogic imagery that emerged full-blown, so to speak, without consciously being willed; vivid visions of people, scenes, objects, known and unfamiliar to the subject. And they were changeful, as if a very private showing of lantern slides were being run through the theatre of the mind' (Segal, p. 324).

From this it would seem that the mind is full of unconscious imagery of which we are ordinarily unaware. And now the aim of researchers is to make it conscious – to bring people to a state in which, so to speak, the unconscious will be luminous to the conscious. In laboratory experiments Dr Green uses certain stimuli to make people aware of the hypnagogic imagery latent in the mind. 'Many gave reports that, were it not for the stimulus, they would not have become aware of these images. One subject reported that the stimulus caused him suddenly to become aware of little pictures in his mind that he did not know were there' (Segal, p. 323).

In terms of brainwaves, in order to become aware of hypnagogic imagery it may be necessary to produce many varieties of brainwave at the same time. This seems to be the opinion of Dr Green. Speaking of a Swami whom he tested, he goes on:

When the Swami produced alpha, he did not cease to produce beta. And when he produced theta, both alpha and beta were retained, each about 50% of the time. Likewise when he produced delta, he was also producing theta, alpha and beta during a relatively high percentage of time. Perhaps this tells us something important. Since alpha is a conscious state, it may be necessary to retain it when theta is produced if one wishes to be aware of the hypnagogic imagery which is often associated with theta.

(Green (5))

From this we get a fascinating picture of the human mind filled with a wealth of imagery that is largely unconscious but that can be brought to consciousness by entering the theta state and receiving some stimulus to enhance awareness and to ensure that in time of theta the alpha and beta rhythms will continue.

Now this may well confirm a very old technique for bringing people to enlightenment. In Zen the stimulus is the blow on the face or the shout or the hard word – or alternatively the gentle falling of the peach blossom or the sound of the temple bell. Whatever it may be, ordinarily some stimulus is necessary to ripen a person's enlightenment and make him aware of what is already in his mind. For he is already enlightened and the stimulus brings to the surface what was there all along. I believe that Jesus too sometimes used the hard word to shock his hearer into self-realization. 'Why do you call me good? None is good but God alone' (Luke 18:19). It should be remembered that according to one Buddhist theory everyone is already enlightened by possession of the Buddha nature. And does not Genesis say that man is created in God's image? Which may be a kind of enlightenment with which man is born. As for the New Testament, it seems to highlight baptism as the great enlightenment. Spiritual training in these cases may be the art of leading a person to the realization of what he already possesses. This may have much to do with the realization and conscious grasp of the hypnagogic imagery that fills the mind with its richness and depth.

One thing that interests Dr Green is the relationship of this hypnagogic, theta imagery to creativity. It is well known that the creativity of poets, artists, writers and scientists is frequently linked to dreams and dream-like states. We have all heard stories about writers waking up in the night and furiously scribbling their great intuitions, or of mathematicians and scientists crying 'Eureka' in the dead of night or at the moment of waking. Elmer Green quotes the chemist Kekulé, who urged his contemporaries: 'Gentlemen, let us learn to dream' (Green (2)).

And again this is not without great relevance for meditation. It is not at all uncommon for religious people to receive deep enlightenment in the twilight zone between waking and sleeping, or at some time in the night. For this is precisely the time when the conscious mind is open to receiving communications from the teeming womb of the unconscious. 'A vision appeared to Paul in the night: a man of Macedonia was standing beseeching him and saying, "Come over to Macedonia and help us." And when he had seen the vision, immediately we sought to go on into Macedonia, concluding that God had called us to preach the gospel to them' (Acts 16:9–10). Was this vision hypnagogic? The Scripture does not say that Paul was asleep; it does not say this was a dream but just that it was 'in the night'. Whatever it was, it was creative and Paul lost no time in following its message.

Dr Green, then, envisages the possibility of training people for creativity through theta. Talented people, by learning how to enter the alpha-theta state, may learn to develop themselves in that area in which they are creative. Artists and writers frequently look for methods to stimulate creativity and here may be one answer. Dr Green writes of 'developing a training programme through which individuals could be helped to develop and sustain those internal states associated with low frequency alpha and theta rhythms in which hypnagogic-like imagery often appears, and of developing a method that would enable us to bring someone in such a state to focused awareness in which he could not only report the imagery but hopefully could learn to manipulate it in a creative way' (Green (2)).

All this brings us to the important and delicate question as to whether and to what extent religious meditation and religious creativity could be developed through biofeedback. Or could religious groups use these machines to teach their aspirants mind-control? to help them produce high-amplitude alpha-theta trains? I must confess that my natural feelings are somewhat jolted by the thought (I always fear the brave new world), but at the same time I cannot help reflecting again on the development of depth psychology – how religious people opposed it and then woke up to its great possibilities, so that now psychological tests are frequently used for screening candidates for monastic or contemplative living. If psychological tests are valid and helpful, why not neurophysiological tests too? If it is true that the alpha-producers are nature's contemplatives, would it not be a good idea to discover them as soon as possible? Quite clearly I am not saying that neurophysiology can tell the whole story (any more than psychology can tell the whole story) and I assume that the deeper things like motivation and faith and love and grace will never show up on the EEG. But granted this, could we make use of biofeedback as we make use of psychology?

In theory I see nothing against it. Only the very practical difficulty that at present biofeedback has not developed sufficiently to be a sure guide about a person's contemplative aptitude. This, I believe, is what most researchers would say. The science is still in its infancy and few would have the confidence to rely on it as a sure norm for the making of big decisions. But what the future holds no one knows. We had better not bury our heads in the sand. It would be sad if religious people were unduly fearful and defensive in the face of modern man's discoveries and explorations into his inner world. If they are open and positive towards scientific trends, they may learn a lot; and they may also help develop and direct scientific discoveries to greater good and greater human fulfilment.

4. *The science of mysticism*

I have called the study of consciousness a new science; but it is probably more correct to say that, like everything else, it evolved over many centuries. The author of Ecclesiastes was not completely off the mark when he observed that there is nothing new under the sun; and some rumblings of a real science (in the rigorously scientific sense) of mysticism have existed in the West for a couple of millennia. Psychoanalysis, the study of brainwaves, trips in inner space and experimentation with drugs are giving renewed vitality to a study that has its roots deep in tradition.

We are so conscious of the catastrophic rift between science and religion that we easily forget about the ancient harmony that existed between them. Monks were in fact the forebears of the modern scientist and their monasteries were, until the Renaissance, the main centres of Western learning – in which no distinction was made between philosophy and what was called natural science. It was a monk, the Venerable Bede, who in the seventh century proposed the notion that the earth was round. Albertus Magnus and his disciple Thomas in the thirteenth century dabbled in speculation about the nature of the universe; Galileo and Copernicus, whoever badly they fared at the hands of the authorities, were educated and nourished by monastic life. Roger Bacon, a Franciscan friar who is responsible for the so-called 'scientific method', wrote that 'the true scientist must subject all things in heaven and under it to experiment. He should blush to find out that he does not know more about the earth than the average person knows.' Then there is Nicolas of Cusa, a mathematician, a mystic and a bishop. And a host of others who devoted their lives to science. I say all this to stress that the scientific approach was deeply rooted in the West. No doubt this was partly a consequence of Yahweh's command to subdue the earth and rule over it.

Now this scientific approach was not without influence on prayer and the mystical states; so that there arose a body of teaching about the development of consciousness in the contemplative life – about various meditational states, about ecstasy, about visions and how to handle them, about the possibility of illusion and so on. Thus were evolved some of the great scientific treatises to which Council Grove referred.

Here I would like to say a word about one great scientist of mysticism, the French Jesuit, Auguste Poulain (1836–1919), whose monumental work *Des Grâces d'Oraison*, written at the beginning of the century, remains a classic. Poulain insisted that he was writing what he called 'descriptive mysticism', that is, getting the facts, analysing them rigorously, sifting the evidence and drawing conclusions. So he read the works of the mystics meticulously (how much loving and patient toil he devoted to this task!), interviewed hundreds of mystics throughout France and reflected on his own mystical experience, which was not small. Great spiritual master that he was, he was convinced that the France of his day abounded in struggling, potential mystics who needed a helping hand. For them he wanted to write a practical book out of his own experience and that of the people he guided and loved. 'For the past forty years', he writes, 'I have made a study of these questions ... I have read large numbers of treatises, ranging from duodecimos to folios. I have questioned at great length numbers of persons possessing the graces of interior prayer, and others who mistakenly thought that they possessed them when in fact they did not. An acquaintance with these last is also helpful' (Poulain, Preface, 3). This last sentence is typical of the shrewd insight that keeps popping up amidst the array of mystical scholarship that fills his pages.

For Poulain, descriptive mysticism depends upon two kinds of materials. First the descriptions found in the great classical writers and secondly the evidence supplied by living persons from their own experience. Both of these are indispensable and they throw light on one another. Indeed he claimed that there are many passages in the writings of the mystics that can only be understood by someone who has had a similar experience. In his research no aspect of mysticism is overlooked. The physical repercussions, the effects upon health, the influence on interpersonal relations, the possible aberrations – all are examined. And then his page upon page of 'extracts' which he culled from his long and painstaking perusal of the Western mystics; these extracts are indeed a veritable gold-mine for the modern researcher in the field of consciousness. As for laboratory experimentation, he seems to have known something about that, according to the scientific milieu of his day. Speaking about ecstasy, for instance, he observes that 'the heart-beat is weak and the breathing so slight that it is difficult even to detect it, *as can be seen from numerous experiments made with great care upon ecstatic persons*' (Poulain, ch. 13, extracts). The italics are mine. What these experiments were he does not say and I have not been able to find out, but it would certainly be interesting to know. For all this situates Tomio Hirai, Elmer Green, Joe Kamiya and other researchers in a long pioneering tradition of meditational scholarship.

Furthermore, for Poulain mysticism, far from being a static science, was constantly in evolution. It had developed slowly through the ages and would continue to develop in the future:

> In the course of the centuries we see that descriptions become more and more accurate. Writers come gradually though very slowly to distinguish, one from the other, states of consciousness which had previously been confused; and they discover better comparisons with which to describe them. In this respect, mysticism partakes in the forward thrust that can be seen in all the descriptive sciences. There is no reason for thinking that there will be no more progress. Our successors will do better than ourselves. And it is in this direction that mysticism has a future.
>
> (Poulain, Preface, 2)

In all this is there not something of a prophetic ring?

For Poulain the writings of St Teresa of Avila in sixteenth-century Spain are a landmark in the development of the mystical consciousness and its scientific study. Teresa was the first, he claims, to analyse minutely the earlier states of consciousness which precede ecstasy; and he constantly appeals to her acute psychological analysis. Asserting that there are two great eras in the development of mysticism, the one before and up to the death of St Teresa of Avila and the other from her death to his own time, he goes on:

> During the first period, mystics devoted their attention only to those facts that stared them in the face: ecstasies, visions of Christ and the saints, and revelations such as those of St Gertrude and St Bridget. But the states of union on the way to ecstasy were more difficult to analyse, as is always the case with more rudimentary things. So their ideas on these states were very vague, their descriptions were brief and hazy and they failed to make distinc-

tions between states of consciousness that were different. For example Blessed Angela of Foligno, whose writings contain such beautiful passages on the subject of raptures and visions, tells us almost nothing about the other states of consciousness. The same is true of Dionysius the Areopagite, Ruysbroeck, and so on. Speaking about the lower phases they were satisfied with such vague remarks as: 'You find that you are taken possession of by a certain sweetness.'

It was St Teresa who was the first to take the trouble to study the states of consciousness below ecstasy under the microscope. Her personal contribution amounts to just this, and in this respect she brought about a true revolution. She has done us a great service, for these states of consciousness are the most common. And in addition to her power of description she had real ability for classification.   (Poulain, ch. 30, 2)

What a sense of history Poulain had! And together with a sense of the past, he had a sense of the future. Mysticism, he laments, has made almost no progress since the time of St Teresa. Scarcely any new facts have been discovered, and authors have been preoccupied with explaining and coordinating what has already been discovered.

Poulain wrote at the beginning of the century. Little did he know that the science of mysticism was on the verge of an earthquake that would shake it to its foundation and make his Teresian revolution look like a tiny tremor. I mean the impact of psychoanalysis, the meeting between Christianity and the religions of the East, the discovery of brainwaves and the popularity of biofeedback and research in drugs. How many new facts now emerge for the West through our knowledge of Ramakrishna and Aurobindo and Dogen! What a contribution is made through the growing knowledge of Buddhist meditation with its divisions and subdivisions of states of consciousness that St Teresa did not know or, at any rate, did not depict. And then the new light thrown on consciousness by the astronauts and space travel. It is true, of course, that Poulain had some glimmering knowledge of psychological and neurological studies and that he was aware of the existence of mysticism in the East. But he was a man of his times, limited by the milieu in which he lived. Many of his observations on these subjects are now out-dated and it is clear that he did not have the spirit of dialogue that we now take for granted.

At the same time, Poulain's research differs from that of contemporary scientists in that it includes a profoundly religious dimension. In the mystics whom he guided and interrogated, the dimensions of faith and charity and ultimate concern were all-important and these are less easily put under the microscope. Here is a whole dimension of mystery that scientific investigation cannot touch. For the traditional mystic the very centre of his practice is purity of motivation in such wise that he seeks the ultimate with what was called 'pure and chaste love'. Now there is no human way of judging another's motivation (hence, 'Judge not, that you be not judged' (Matthew 7:1)) nor can we have certainty about our own. That is why we come up against mystery in a love affair where the beloved is 'the mountains, the solitary wooded valleys, strange islands . . . silent music'. There is no way of measuring and programming any love, much less divine love.

Again there is bound to be awful mystery in an exercise that is built on the belief that ultimate reality is dynamic, that it moves towards us as we move towards it, that it searches us out before we go in search of it. And the mystics directed by Poulain believed not only that ultimate reality is dynamic but that it has a face and a heart and a name. The whole mystical tradition in which Poulain stands is based on the Johannine sentence, 'We love [God], because he first loved us' (1 John 4:19). That is to say, there is a prior action of ultimate reality inviting man to contemplative wisdom; and the mystical path is an answer to this call. This means that there is another actor in the drama and that we must, in consequence, reckon with the action of his love. This is technically called 'grace'.

Something like 'grace' has to be taken into account in the lives of all the great mystics whether they be Jewish, Christian, Hindu or Buddhist. Assuredly Zen Buddhism rejects such an idea and glories in its self-reliance, called in Japanese *jiriki*. Yet even here masters sometimes get second thoughts. At one of our Zen-Christian dialogues, an old and highly esteemed master compared enlightenment to the chicken emerging from the shell. Push as it may, he said, the tiny chick cannot break out to freedom unless the mother pecks at the shell from outside. This, he went on, is equivalent to what Christians call grace. Something similar is found in the famous Oxherding pictures which describe the Zen journey to awakening. Here the searcher must see the footprints and feel the attraction of the ox before he can set out on his arduous journey.

The point I make here is that unless this mysterious religious dimension is taken into account in mystical experience and deep meditation, the picture will be falsified. Quite certainly this is the case in Jewish and Christian prayer. Here we are always confronted with an incalculable element of mystery because two free agents are somehow involved.

To preserve the balance between the strictly scientific dimension on the one hand and the religious and theological on the other is far from easy. Though Poulain's orthodoxy was never questioned, there was a rival school of speculative theologians who, looking askance at his methodology, approached mysticism almost exclusively from the standpoint of scripture and dogma. Though this approach has great validity (which Poulain explicitly admits), it can suffer from the disadvantage of talking about what the mystics *should* experience or what the theologian would like them to experience rather than what, in fact, they do experience. Moreover, theologians of this school spoke a language and used a terminology that other poor mortals, including the scientists, were unlikely to understand. Most disastrous of all, it was this school of theology that prevailed in the seminaries, wrote the text-books, got the *imprimatur* and influenced theological thinking. Consequently, when the modern flood of interest in oriental mysticism and states of consciousness swept into the West, the mystical theologians had already lost contact. What they said did not sound very meaningful; and many scientists working in the field of consciousness have dismissed the Western mystics as shallow or irrelevant. Now the theologian is faced with the unenviable task of picking up the broken pieces.

Poulain was clearly a man in advance of his times. If I were asked to define his role, I would call him not a scientist but a mystical theologian open to dialogue with science and with the world of his day. I call him a theologian because his prime interest was in the divine action on the lives of those whom he directed. In other words his first interest was the working of grace and of God's self-communication to man, about which he learned from scripture, from tradition, from the writings of the mystics, from the intimate disclosures of those he directed and from the action of the Spirit in his own heart. But he was also keenly aware of the vital importance of what we now call neurophysiology and psychophysiology. He was shrewd enough to see that just as the moral theologian cannot neglect psychology, economics, sociology and the other sciences that border on his specialization, so the mystical theologian cannot neglect the sciences that touch his field. In short he saw the necessity of the interdisciplinary approach; and in this sense he points to the path along which future research in mysticism must walk. This is the path of dialogue.

For the future of mysticism may well be in the balance. It could be bright or it could be pretty dark because of the enormous spiritual potential that will be unleashed as the human race becomes progressively more mystical. Let me here look on the bright side. Mysticism can be a unifying factor in a world searching for wholeness. Already it has done much towards bringing together the great religions. We now see that Hindus and Christians, Buddhists and Jews can dialogue and understand one another better at the level of mystical experience than at the level of philosophy. But mysticism can be a meeting ground not only for believers in the various religions but also for scientists and religionists. These latter approach the problem at the level of mystery, of ultimate concern, of transcendence; and they can dialogue with those who approach the same problem as psychologists,p sychiatrists, neurologists, physicists, biologists and the rest. Who doubts that we have great need of some unifying science? And mysticism may well be the answer.

PART II

CONSCIOUSNESS

5. *Initiation*

In the meditation of the great religions one makes progress by going beyond thought, beyond concepts, beyond images, beyond reasoning, thus entering a deeper state of consciousness or enhanced awareness that is characterized by profound silence. This is the *silentium mysticum*. It is a state of consciousness in which there may be no words or images. Or if there are words, they spring from the depth of one's being and are not borrowed from books or outside sources; and if there are images, these again will be from within, more in the nature of hypnagogic imagery than that which we create by conscious visualization. Frequently this state of silent unification will be filled with peace; but it may at times be dry and even painfully filled with anguish. It is a silence that probably differs considerably according to the faith of the meditator, and it goes by different names in the different religious traditions. In Sanskrit the generic word *samadhi* is used, though this word has a wide variety of meanings; in Christianity it is called *contemplation* or, in its earlier stages, *the prayer of quiet*. In Zen it is called *san'mai*, which is a Japanese rendering of *samadhi*. Elsewhere it is called one-pointedness. Physiologically speaking, it seems to be characterized by high-amplitude alpha brainwaves. The breathing slows down (some Buddhists measure the depth of their *samadhi* by the rate of breathing), as also do the heart-rate and general metabolism, while the consciousness is greatly expanded.

There are so many divisions and subdivisions of mystical silence that researchers in consciousness have no vocabulary that will encompass the whole complex thing and they are anxiously looking for one. Perhaps that is the reason for their growing interest in mysticism and the mystics. The problem is by no means easy because it is impossible to speak accurately about altered or expanded states of consciousness in terms taken from ordinary, normal, waking consciousness. It is like denizens of two different worlds or universes trying to communicate with one another. Hence mystics usually resort to silence or to symbolism. In the West the Church fathers speak of Moses climbing the mountain to meet Yahweh in the dark

cloud of unknowing or of Mary Magdalen sitting silently at the feet
of Christ; while St Teresa speaks of the successive interior mansions
into which one enters to meet the king at the deepest centre. It
takes the scientist some time to get accustomed to such language.
And the matter becomes all the more complex when we reflect that
among the many kinds of interior silence are some that are unhealthy.
It is well said in Japan that any clown can tell the difference between
wise talk and foolish talk; but it takes a good master to distinguish
between wise silence and foolish silence.

The transition from the rational, wordy consciousness to a deeper,
mystical and intuitive consciousness has been the object of considerable psychological study in recent times. What precisely happens in
the process of passing from an excited state characterized by beta to
a relaxed awareness in which alpha predominates? One of the more
widely accepted explanations is the so-called filter theory (Naranjo,
pp. 170 ff.). According to this, the brain and nervous system are
fitted with restrictive filters or barriers of some kind which prevent
total reality from entering consciousness, only permitting the
entrance of such knowledge as man needs for biological survival.
These filters are nothing less than a repressive mechanism calculated
to impede the inrush of knowledge that would otherwise overwhelm
and break us. In this sense they are a sort of protective screen:
humankind, unable to bear too much reality, must find some way of
blocking things out.

But these protective barriers, this theory continues, can be removed
so that more knowledge enters, thus expanding the mind. Probably
one way of removing them is by the intake of drugs. Or they are
perhaps broken down in certain forms of mental illness. In these
cases, the floodgates are opened and reality rushes in, often with
horrendous and traumatic consequences. Or again, some people may
be born with less restrictive filters; and these are the 'psychics', who
are open to telepathy, clairvoyance and other parapsychological
sources of information. Meditation is also a human and natural way
of opening the filters, welcoming the inflow of reality, and expanding
the mind. It is a gradual process, a daily practice, in which the filters
or barriers are slowly lifted to allow an almost imperceptible inflow
of greater reality into the intuitive consciousness -- though this
unhurried process may, at times, give way to a sudden collapse of
barriers that causes massive enlightenment or mystical experience.
In all this, meditation is safer than drugs because the meditator, if

properly instructed and guided, can integrate the new knowledge and preserve his equilibrium. This point I will take up again in a later chapter.

Let me now mention some ways, common to many religious traditions, by which one enters the unitive silence that lies beyond thought. These are techniques for restricting or rejecting the rational consciousness, thus allowing the deeper, intuitive consciousness to rise to the surface of the mind.

Zen Buddhism nurtures the intuitive consciousness by a radical rejection of the rational. Conceptualization of any kind is jettisoned. Here are the words of an ancient Zen master:

> Conceptualization is a deadly hindrance to the Zen yogis, more injurious than poisonous snakes or fierce beasts . . . Brilliant and intellectual persons always abide in the cave of conceptualization; they can never get away from it in all their activities. As months and years pass they become more deeply engulfed in it. Unknowingly the mind and conceptualization gradually become of a piece. Even if one wants to get away from it, he finds it impossible. Therefore, I say, poisonous snakes and beasts are avoidable, but there is no way to escape from mental conceptualization.
>
> (Chang, p. 86)

attending to God

In Zen, then, one rejects reason, thought and imagery in order to enter the deeper area of *san'mai*. In *Soto* Zen this is ordinarily done by attention to, or concentration on, the breathing, which has the effect of brushing away all thoughts and images, and of restricting consciousness to the one single process of breathing. When conceptual thought is thus abandoned, intuitive consciousness begins to rise to the surface, giving one a sense of well-being and of interior integration.

In the Western mystical tradition as it evolved since the sixteenth century, it was usual to begin meditation with a certain amount of reasoning and thinking about the scriptures, about the life of Christ and so on. This was called 'discursive prayer' and in time it was simplified to the process of repeating aspirations (this was technically called 'affective prayer') and finally to the repetition of one aspiration and the entrance into intuitive silence. This last stage was called 'the prayer of simplicity' or 'the prayer of the heart' or 'the prayer of simple regard' or 'acquired contemplation'.

It will be noticed that in the West (unlike Zen Buddhism) rational thinking, far from being rejected, is the very road that leads to intuition. Perhaps there is here a valuable Western insight, based on an intensely incarnational view of life: the whole man should be involved in meditation – the whole man with his rational and intuitive capacities. Only by developing and appreciating and then *going beyond* the rational can he reach the intuitive in an integral way. I.believe this approach to meditation produced men who were great in reason and great in intuition. I mean men like Augustine and Thomas Aquinas and Bergson and Teilhard.

But let me now continue to describe some techniques for entering into *samadhi*.

One of the most common is the repetition of a *mantra* or sacred word. This is the method employed in transcendental meditation, where one simply adopts a comfortable position (though it is advised that the back be kept straight), closes one's eyes and repeats interiorly the *mantra* in a passive way. What is important is not the meaning (most practitioners do not know what their *mantra* means) but the vibrations, which have the effect of leading one into deeper and more subtle layers of consciousness and of psychic life. And all this without the rigours of Zen. The most famous Indian *mantra* is OM. In Japan, while Zen was always for an élite, the repetition of the *mantra* Namu Amida Butsu[1] had enormous influence on the masses of believers in Pure Land Buddhism. In Christianity the word 'Jesus' is a very traditional '*mantra*', but others, too, were used. Here is the advice of a fourteenth-century English mystic on the use of the *mantra*:

If you want to gather all your desire into one simple word that the mind can easily retain, choose a short word rather than a long one. A one syllable word such as 'God' or 'love' is best. But choose one that is meaningful to you. Then fix it in your mind so that it will remain there come what may. This word will be your defense in conflict and in peace. Use it to beat upon the cloud of darkness above you and subdue all distractions, consigning them to the cloud of forgetting beneath you. Should some thought go on annoying you, demanding to know what you are doing, answer with this one word alone. If your mind begins to intellectualize

---

[1] 'Honour to the Buddha, Amida.'

over the meaning and connotations of this little word, remind
yourself that its value lies in its simplicity. Do this and I assure
you these thoughts will vanish. Why? Because you have refused
to develop them with arguing.   (Johnston (1), ch. 7)

For this author, the *mantra* is a kind of weapon for warding off
reasoning, thinking and conceptualization. By it, too, the horizon of
rational consciousness is narrowed and prepared for the breakthrough. Interesting is his paradoxical advice to choose a meaningful
word and yet not to bother about the meaning. Anyone who uses a
mantra will tell you that his word is extremely meaningful but he
doesn't bother about the meaning. Perhaps this is because a *mantra*
is above all symbolic – it points to something other than itself.

It should be noted that in the use of the *mantra*, monotony, far
from being an obstacle to enlightenment, is central to the practice.
This is because monotony is another way of restricting the reflective
consciousness. If things become too interesting at the rational,
discursive level, one may want to stay there; one may cling to one's
interesting thoughts, losing the desire to break through to something
deeper. If, on the other hand, monotony predominates at the
discursive level, the intuitive is allowed to act. Hence the monotonous
repetition of litanies in the West:

> Ora pro nobis
> Ora pro nobis
> Ora pro nobis

Or again, the constant recitation of the Ave Maria in the rosary.
These are ways of introducing people to mind-expansion and
enlightenment.

Somewhat similar to the use of the *mantra* is the recitation of the
sutras in Buddhism and of the Gregorian chant in Christianity.
Here also rhythm and monotony are important elements in introducing the chanter to the prayer of quiet. That is one reason why
the psalms were recited in common by the monks for centuries. But
again it is interesting to see that whereas Japanese Buddhists
frequently recited Chinese sutras which they did not understand,
Western monasticism never rejected meaning. It aimed at going
beyond the rational meaning to a deeper, primordial and transcendent meaning. That is to say, it went beyond wordy meaning at

the discursive level to find deeper meaning in wordless wisdom.

Yet another way of restricting rational consciousness and entering a deeper level of mind is the use of the *mandala*. This is a visual image, sometimes very complex and sometimes just a simple circle, on which one fixes one's gaze. Its use is common in the Tibetan tradition of esoteric Buddhism. Within Christianity I believe the principal '*mandala*' has been the crucifix, upon which people have fixed their gaze for hours and hours without words or images or thoughts of conceptualization and in this way have broken through to enlightenment and resurrection. Or again, the tabernacle has been a *mandala* upon which simple people, who, of course, never heard the word *mandala*, have fixed their eyes in silent expansion of consciousness or *samadhi* or one-pointedness or the prayer of quiet.

Another way of enhancing awareness, found in Zen, is the process of listening to every sound. There is a *koan kikunushi* usually translated, 'Who is the master that is hearing?' Using this *koan*, one listens to every single sound, all the time asking who is the subject that hears. In this way, it is said, the bodhisattva, Kannon, found enlightenment. Like the other *koan*, it restricts rational consciousness and forces the mind to a breakthrough. Again, in Christianity I believe that the crucifix, besides being a *mandala*, is a *koan*. Paul makes this pretty clear when he says in Corinthians I that Christ crucified is a scandal and a stumbling block, but once understood, it is wisdom. Quite a good definition of the *koan* from Paul.

I have insisted that in all these methods the technique is that of limiting rational consciousness to one process. That is to say, the stream of consciousness being restricted, the mind is forced to work vertically downwards, and is in consequence expanded. The same effect, however, is sometimes achieved simply by fixing the mind on God without any of the above techniques. Here is the clear and direct advice of the author of *The Cloud*:

> This is what you are to do: lift up your heart to the Lord, with a gentle stirring of love desiring him for his own sake and not for his gifts. Centre all your attention and desire on him and let this be the sole concern of your mind and heart. Do all in your power to forget everything else, keeping your thoughts and desires free from involvement with any of God's creatures or their affairs whether general or particular.   (Johnston (1), ch. 3)

This seemingly simple advice cannot be put into practice, however, without tremendous control of the mind. In fact one generally cannot do it without training in the other methods for entering *samadhi* already referred to.

Yet another way to the silent state of consciousness and one that deserves special mention, is the process of visualization. This can be of many kinds, as may be evident from what has already been said about laboratory experiments in hypnagogic imagery. One can close one's eyes and imagine a scene – or, on the other hand, one may suddenly and unexpectedly become aware of dream-like imagery that is already present in the mind. This latter is clearly of another order, enacted at a different level of consciousness from the ordinary process of conjuring up a scene. In short, there is a type of visualization that destroys alpha (and on this point I quoted Dr Kamiya in an earlier chapter) and there is a visualization that springs from alpha and more often from the combination of alpha and theta.

A Buddhist monk told me that in his sect (he belonged to esoteric Buddhism) one of the best ways to enlightenment was to visualize the Buddha with which you wish to identify, be it Amida or Kannon or whatever – and in this way one loses self and becomes a Buddha. He told me that some monks were so good at visualization that they could actually bring themselves to see the Buddha of their choice. He confessed, however, that this kind of visualization did not appeal to him personally and that he was not expert in its practice.

Yet deeper than all this, and deeper than hypnagogic imagery, is an area of psychic life that is associated with what Western mystics have called 'the interior senses'. Here is seeing and feeling and hearing and touching of a different kind and in a new dimension. St Teresa, for example, writes: 'One day, when I was at prayer . . . I saw Christ at my side – or to put it better, I was conscious of him, *for I saw nothing with the eyes of the body or of the soul*' (Teresa (1), ch. 27). This experience, frequent in the life of Teresa, differs from the Buddhist visualization I have spoken about in that it is not conjured up or deliberately fostered. It is something that just happens, a spontaneous activity arising from within. Moreover it differs from the hypnagogic imagery that appears in the alpha-theta experimentation of Dr Elmer Green. This latter was described by subjects as being vivid like lantern-slides, whereas Teresa's images are not seen at all.

What St Teresa and the mystics say about seeing is paralleled by

Locutions

The New Theology — being called

what they say about hearing. Locutions can be heard at many levels, not only at the level of the bodily ears. I believe that the prophets of Israel heard locutions of this kind. They really heard something or someone speaking in the depths of their being; they really heard themselves called by name, 'Abraham, Abraham . . .'; but the voice of Yahweh did not impinge upon their bodily ears like the vibrations of a human voice. Something much deeper was going on. 'Now the word of the Lord came to me saying, "Before I formed you in the womb I knew you . . ." ' (Jeremiah 1:4–5). Or with Paul: 'And I know that this man was caught up into Paradise . . . and he heard things that cannot be told, which men may not utter' (2 Corinthians 12:3). I do not believe that Paul heard a human voice or that sonic vibrations struck his ears. He was beyond all this, hearing beyond hearing.

Today, also, locutions are by no means unusual with people who meditate deeply. And the most common is still the sound of one's name being called in the core of the being without reference to the physical ears. 'Do not be afraid, Mary . . .' (Luke 1:30). In the Hebrew tradition the name has marvellous significance and penetrates to the innermost self. And the experience of being thus called by Yahweh in a personal, loving encounter is central to the Bible. Needless to say, in all this the name is not one's ordinary given name. Rather does one have the sense of being called by that which is of one's personal essence. It is something that cannot be reiterated in human speech. One just knows it and, in a sense, remembers it in so far as it was a *creative word* and one knows the self it created.

It will be readily seen that we are here dealing with a whole area of psychic life ordinarily dormant but opened up through meditation. The mystics claim that they see and hear and smell and touch and embrace in a way that is totally different from the ordinary experience of man. How astonishing their talk of being inebriated with wine and of the kiss of love and all the rest!

Poulain tackles the problem of interior senses in his usual scientific and matter-of-fact way with the question: 'Has the soul intellectual, spiritual senses which in some way resemble the bodily senses so that in an analogous manner and in different ways she can perceive the presence of pure spirits and of God in particular?' (Poulain, ch. 6) He answers in the affirmative and then sums up:

the sense of being called by that which is of one's personal essence.

The physiognomy of the mystic union can be described in the following way: during the union, when it is not too deep, we are like a man seated beside one of his friends in darkness and in silence. He does not *see* him therefore, he does not *hear* him; he only *feels* that he is there by the sense of touch since he is holding his hand. And so he goes on thinking about him and loving him.

The material touch may, as it increases in strength, turn into a clasping and an embrace. It is the same with the spiritual touch. In the prayer of quiet, when it is not very strong, it is a simple drinking in which is tranquilly enjoyed. But sometimes the two spirits embrace one another, which is to say that sudden and affectionate claspings between them take place.

This abundance of grace is not, I believe, common with beginners; and when they at length come to experience it, it is at first only for a few seconds at a time. Afterwards, if they were to try to reproduce this special impression they could not do so.

(Poulain, ch. 6)

It goes without saying that we are here confronted with a psychic dimension which is of the utmost importance for the full understanding of man. A century ago some people were content to look on mystics like St Teresa as oddballs; others preferred to think that they received special powers from God. Now I believe we can say that they were normal people, making use of faculties inherent in man though the majority of people are unaware of their existence. How little of our potentiality we use! It may well be that, as Bergson observed, the mystics are in the vanguard of evolution, men and women before their time – what they experienced may well be an ordinary thing in the years that lie ahead. Be that as it may, I do not believe that these interior faculties are purely spiritual – Platonic rejections of matter. I prefer to use the Teilhardian terminology of 'spiritualized matter' and to think of them as highly developed human activities. Probably hominization will not be complete until these faculties are actuated and man is fully alive. But I also believe that the interior senses will never be brought into play until one is able to transcend the monopolizing power of the exterior sense. That there is a tremendous need for renunciation all the mystics agree. But more about this later.

I am aware of the paradoxical nature of everything that I here say. On the one hand I began with the assertion that mysticism is an

mysticism is an entrance into
silence – it is an altered state of
consciousness full of
paradoxes

64   *Silent Music*

entrance into silence and then I spoke about words; I said it was
imageless and then I spoke about seeing. Yet this is precisely the
language of the mystics. They talk about emptiness, darkness, the
void, the nothingness, using a string of words that suggest total
negativity; and then, in the next breath, they begin to describe it in
terms that are rich, joyful, beautiful, erotic. It would seem that the
void and the nothingness of the mystics is not a repelling spiritual
poverty but an ocean of indescribable wealth, a treasure-house of
unearthly beauty. Nothing is all; darkness is light; suffering is joy.
How this can be is difficult to say unless one has had some experience.
Then the whole thing seems obvious. All I can do here is repeat what
was said earlier; namely, that this is an expanded or altered state of
consciousness and to explain it in terms of the ordinary day-to-day
consciousness that makes up our language is almost impossible.
Language from one state of consciousness just does not fit the other.
This also explains why mystics will say that everything is one and yet
that everything is not one. At one level of consciousness we see the
unity and at another we see the diversity. Both statements, I believe,
are true; both express something about reality. And modern Western
man simply must learn to accept the validity of paradox if he wants
to understand.

Paradox

I have described some ways and techniques for expanding the mind
and entering into mystical silence. More could be mentioned. There
is fasting, for instance, which has the effect of expanding consciousness. The precise repercussions of fasting – its influence on the flow
of blood to the brain and the general metabolism – are now being
studied, and the forthcoming conclusions will surely be of the utmost
significance for the meditation movement. Or again, in some religious
traditions dancing leads to one-pointedness, as in the case of the
famous whirling dervishes.

These are all techniques. But let me now hasten to add that in
deep meditation there is more than technique. In the heart of the
man of good will, whatever his religious affiliation, I believe that the
Spirit is at work. And this is the incalculable element which escapes
definition and which cannot be circumscribed. I further believe that
faith in the action of the Spirit deepens meditation immeasurably. If
we believe in something beyond self, beyond consciousness, beyond
our own spiritual faculties however refined, then meditation enters
a new dimension.

faith in the action of the Spirit
deepens meditation

Mention of the Spirit reminds me of yet another way to enlightenment which many of my readers will undoubtedly have experienced. This is the way of love.

If two or more people love one another deeply, they may be brought to the profound level of awareness and mind-expansion that the great religions speak of. They may come to that *samadhi* in which no words are necessary because their intimacy is not built on words. And the stronger the love, the more profound will be the silence and the deeper will be the enlightenment. Furthermore, if this love goes to the core of their being, it brings a realization of something more than the people involved – it brings a consciousness of the all; it contains an element of universality. This, I believe, is a truly religious experience, very central to the Bible, which tells us that 'he who loves . . . knows God . . . for God is love' (1 John 4:7–8). The Bible does not say that he who *loves God* knows God; it says that he who *loves* knows God. And if this is so, human love must be the supreme way to *samadhi*, to enlightenment, to God. Nor need this, in the case of man-woman love, be sexual in the physical sense. Psychologists will surely agree with me that, ideally speaking, sexual intercourse is an expression of something deeper – and it is this deeper thing that I am talking about here. It may, of course, be expressed sexually or it may not. That depends on the persons, their relationship and their circumstances. In itself it is a deeply spiritual communication, going beyond the emotional and intellectual to the intuitive consciousness. It is one of the most human roads to contemplation.

That love leads to enlightenment is a recurrent theme in the Western mystics. Love they compare to a candle which gives light and enables us to see both our own misery and God's great goodness. No doubt it helps us to see the great goodness of other people too – if we love them, we are enlightened about their value and worth and goodness. St Teresa says quite simply of the prayer of quiet that it is not necessary to know much (in the rational sense) but to love much. That love should lead to enlightenment is easy to comprehend when we recall that the essence of the oriental awakening is the loss of self (called *muga* in Japanese and *anatta* in Pali) and that self is radically lost through love. Aquinas calls love 'ecstatic' because it, so to speak, goes out and lives in what it loves. Perhaps his idea is best expressed in poetry like that of St John of the Cross who exclaims:

'O life, how canst thou endure, since thou livest not where thou livest?' – as if to say that his life has gone out from himself to live in the beloved and he wonders that it can continue to dwell in his breast. And then there are the beautiful words of the poet-martyr Robert Southwell, 'Not where I breathe, but where I love, I live!' Here is a dramatic loss of self through love.

Needless to say, the love that leads to enlightenment is of a very high order. It is the love Teilhard speaks of when he declares that at the level of the person union differentiates. Teilhard makes a good distinction between union and absorption. Two people can be fascinated with one another, lost in one another, absorbed in one another – in total oblivion of everything, even of themselves. Such love is adolescent. It may be a stage in growth towards maturity, but it is still self-centred. Love of union, on the other hand, differentiates in that the two people find their true selves, are transparent to one another, live in one another, and are in consequence opened up to the all. Early in his life, Teilhard was faced with the awful mystical dilemma of how to become the other while remaining one's self; and here he found the solution: union between persons differentiates. It is this person-to-person love that is a road to enlightenment.

Union differentiates! Insufferable paradox you will say. Yes, but we are learning to think in paradox. And we must think in paradox if we want to reach enlightenment. To the person with experience of love the paradox will present no difficulty. 'Give me one who loves', says Augustine, 'and he will understand what I say . . .'

To enter the mystical path through love may sound attractive and easy. Attractive indeed it is; but not easy. Anyone can gaze for hours at a flower or a flame or a *mandala* with the safe assurance that it won't hit back, it won't hurt him, it won't betray him. He can be united with a flower in great security. But with other persons much more is involved. The fear of being hurt, or betrayed, or unrequited – the fact that free persons are interacting on one another. All this makes for deeper purification, deeper anguish, deeper love and, in consequence, deeper enlightenment.

Moreover the enlightenment that comes from love is necessarily incarnational. It involves us in society and never cuts us off from reality. This point is worth noting. Talk of altered states of consciousness, of interior senses, of ecstasy and the rest might give us the impression that meditators and mystics are divorced from reality – whereas the contrary is true. Gandhi, Martin Luther King, Dag

[handwritten margin note:] love between persons differentiates – leaves to the all

[handwritten note at bottom:] enlightenment that comes from love is incarnational

Hammarskjöld, Thomas Merton still speak to us of a mystical life integrated with service to men. And apart from these giants there are a host of unknown people who integrate mysticism with the hum-drum waking consciousness and with daily living in community or family. This is important. For it is mainly through this ordinary life in society that we can distinguish sound mysticism from some forms of mental illness and from Gnostic meanderings in a phantasmal world of inner space.

My contention throughout this book is that this love is the essence of the deepest meditation. To try to understand Teresa or Poulain or Ramakrishna or Martin Buber while neglecting it would be to falsify the whole picture. This love can exist between people of the same sex ('Simon, son of John, do you love me . . . ?' (John 21:15)), or between those of the opposite sex, or it can be love for a com-munity. My point is that whether one recites the *mantra* or gazes at the *mandala* or wrestles with the *koan*, the whole process should be undergirded by love if the enlightenment is to go the whole way. In fact, the development of meditation can be compared to a love affair. When two people begin to love, they may chatter and use words a good deal; but as their intimacy grows, words become less necessary and are even superfluous. The two maintain a total and unitive silence, enjoying one another's presence in love. And the same holds true when the beloved is 'the mountains, the solitary wooded valleys, strange islands . . . silent music'.

6. *The road to ecstasy*

Writers in many of the religious traditions have depicted successive states of consciousness which the meditator passes through on his way to enlightenment or resurrection. In the West, one of the best known of these is St Teresa of Avila whose *Interior Castle* will always be a classic and a source-book for the researcher in states of consciousness. In this book Teresa divides the interior odyssey into seven mansions of which the last four are deeply mystical and of great relevance today. The soul is a castle in the interior of which dwells the king; and the meditator, at the invitation of this king, makes a journey into inner space to find him enthroned at the centre of the soul.

The experience of St Teresa tallies with that of many Western mystics; so let me describe this journey into inner space, once more following the lead of Auguste Poulain. Relying mainly, but by no means exclusively, on St Teresa, Poulain divides the mystic states of consciousness broadly into four.

The first is the prayer of quiet:

> This comes abruptly and unexpectedly. You are suddenly possessed by an unusual state of recollection which you cannot help but notice. You are overtaken by a divine wave that fills you through and through. You remain motionless beneath the influence of this sweet impression. And then it all disappears with the same suddenness. Beginners are surprised at this, for they find that they are overtaken by something that they cannot completely understand. But they surrender themselves to this inclination because they realize at once that it is something holy. They postpone to a later date the task of examining it more closely. (Poulain, ch. 16)

This, then, is the initial awakening. In the mystical life it is a moment of the greatest significance, which Teresa describes in great detail. If one were to take this experience lightly or forget it, or misunderstand it, a priceless treasure might well be lost. Buddhists say something similar. A Buddhist monk once asked me bluntly if I could recall the moment when I first entered *samadhi*. I was taken aback by the abruptness of the question which seemed like an invasion of privacy. He then told me that this question was frequently asked in the monastery where he did his training. It was considered helpful for a monk to reflect on the first stage of his spiritual journey.

If one values these moments of enlightenment and fosters them, this state of consciousness will become habitual. In general it can be said that the mystical life consists of peak experiences which eventually become plateaus. This state, initially surprising and abrupt, becomes the ordinary thing. So says Poulain:

> Finally a time comes when the prayer of quiet is not only very frequent but *habitual*. Now we have it as our state whenever we want it. It will occur outside the time of prayer and whenever the thought of God is presented, as for example in conversation. This is enough for us to be seized by the divine action. If this action is powerful, then we may find that it interferes with our occupation, but usually it all disappears quickly. At other times the divine action seems to have a mute influence which continues in the midst of a busy life. (Poulain, ch. 16)

From this it can be seen that meditation is not just something that one practises night and morning. It perdures. It comes to take over one's life. If a person's *samadhi* only arises in time formally devoted to meditation, this indicates that it is still superficial. Zen meditators will frequently say that Zen is walking, Zen is eating, Zen is sleeping, Zen is life . . . And all the traditions teach much the same thing.

In this first state of consciousness, which we have called the prayer of quiet, two levels of psychic life are at work simultaneously. The upper, imaginative level may be roaming and romping and roaring wildly (St Teresa calls it 'the fool of the house') while the deeper level is silently unified and at peace. In the stage which follows, however, known as 'the prayer of union', a unification of these two levels is effected so that one is 'without distraction' – two worlds are, so to speak, united. In this way the personality is greatly integrated in a state of consciousness which Poulain describes as follows:

> It is a mystical union of such power that the soul is totally occupied with the divine object. In short, there are no distractions. Yet the

senses keep on acting, at any rate partially acting. Furthermore, with a certain amount of effort it is possible to re-establish relations with the external world, to make movements and to come out of this state. (Poulain, ch. 17)

Poulain then quotes St Teresa, who in her fifth mansion compares the prayer of quiet to drowsiness and the prayer of union to sleep. One is asleep as regards the world and oneself, and during the brief time that this state lasts, one is deprived of all feeling and unable to think discursively.

The third stage is ecstasy. To understand this it should be noted that from the outset of the prayer of quiet the meditator has had some difficulty in using his discursive faculties and he eventually finds himself in a situation technically known as the 'ligature' because he is as it were 'bound'. 'In the prayer of quiet', writes Poulain, 'the ligature does not constitute a complete impossibility. Thus we can begin to formulate a vocal prayer such as the Paternoster. But after a few words some unknown and secret force hinders us. We hesitate and we stammer. By a renewed effort, however, we can start again; and so it goes on. If we attempted to continue the struggle we would soon be very tired. The right thing to do is to resign ourselves' (Poulain, ch. 14).

As the union deepens, however, the ligature grows and develops into ecstasy, which is 'a state which not only at the beginning but during its whole course contains two essential elements. The first, which is interior and invisible, is a very keen attention to some religious object; the second, which is corporeal and visible, is the alienation of the sensible faculties' (Poulain, ch. 13). As for the description of ecstasy:

Ecstasy is found when the divine action is of great force, and all communication with the external sense is broken, or almost entirely so. We are no longer able to move, at least voluntarily, nor are we able to come out of our prayer at will.[1]

(Poulain, ch. 3)

[1] Poulain devotes a good deal of space to describing ecstasy. See chapter 13:

(1) *The senses* cease to act, or they convey only a confused knowledge . . .

(2) As a general rule, *the limbs* become motionless, and it becomes

simple ecstasy
rapture
flight of the spirit
union

There are degrees or grades of ecstasy. 'Simple ecstasy' comes upon the meditator slowly. 'Rapture' is sudden and violent. Then there is 'flight of the spirit' in which St Teresa affirms that she does not know whether or not the spirit remains in her body. Her words remind one of Paul – 'whether in the body or out of the body I do not know, God knows' (2 Corinthians 12:2). The secrets and revelations that Paul refers to in this state are shared by other ecstatics. About rapture St Teresa affirms that it is very alarming at first, that often it is irresistible (though simple ecstasy can be resisted) and that one remains in the position in which one was before the ecstasy came. One comes out of the ecstasy at the command of a superior or some authorized person – this was called 'the recall'.

Poulain's fourth and final state of consciousness is the 'transform-

---

impossible to speak or to walk or to make any gesture . . .

(3) *The respiration* almost ceases; sometimes it seems to cease altogether. The same is true for the heart-beats as well as for the pulse. In all these things there are differences of degree, according to the depth of the experience. Sometimes at certain moments there has been reason to fear that death has supervened.

(4) *The vital heat* seems to disappear and a coldness sets in at the extremities.

To sum up, everything seems as if the soul were losing in vital strength . . .

Later in the same chapter Poulain describes the effects of ecstasy in greater detail. For example:

The effect upon the eyes. It is only possible to observe this properly if, while the body is motionless, the eyes remain wide open and fixed. Several people have told me that they then saw the things around them as though they were veiled in a white mist. It is something like an evenly dispersed fog, or like the smoke that rises from incense . . .

And again:

In the case of ecstasy we sometimes come across the following phenomena in regard to the body:
(1) The body rises up into the air. This is called *levitation*;
(2) Or it is surrounded by a luminous *aureole*;
(3) Or it emits a sweet fragrance.

This chapter of Poulain should be interesting for the researcher in the psychophysiology of meditation.

ing union', called by Teresa the 'spiritual marriage'. There is no
ecstasy here because, once again, the peak has become a plateau. The
meditator, now accustomed to the powerful inflow of spirit, is able
to control it. Hence no more suspension of the sensible faculties, no
more loss of control, no more ligature, and in place of these a great
freedom to act and to work and to love. This in some ways resembles
the Zen 'return to the market-place', a stage in which the enlightened
person comes back to ordinary life to redeem all sentient beings. In
Zen, it may be remembered, there is the first stage, in which trees
are trees, rivers are rivers and mountains are mountains; followed by
a second stage, in which trees are rivers, and rivers are mountains,
and mountains are trees; only to be followed by the final stage of
enlightenment, when once again trees are trees, rivers are rivers and
mountains are mountains. In some such way, the transforming
union is a completely ordinary and normal state in which, however,
one is moved and motivated by something deeper than oneself.
Hence the Christian mystics' constant appeal to the Pauline, 'It is
no longer I who live, but Christ who lives in me' (Galatians 2:20).
One is moved by the Christ within who speaks and acts and loves
and blesses and cries out, 'Abba! Father!' (Galatians 4:6) This is the
peak-point of hominization when one has found one's true self and,
in the case of Christians, has found one's true self in Christ. St John
of the Cross puts it well when he says that at the beginning one sees
the Creator through the creatures but at the end one sees the creatures
through the Creator.

In the above four stages of mysticism I have followed Poulain. It is
interesting to note, however, that the majority of his contemporaries
had different views on the role of ecstasy. The French Jesuit, Joseph
de Guibert (1877–1942), for example, maintained that ecstasy was
by no means an integral part of the mystical ascent. It was, he claimed,
simply a consequence arising from the weakness of the human
organism unable to stand such a powerful inflow of spirit without
losing the use of its physical and psychological faculties. Consequently, the person who was physically and psychologically strong
would undergo no ligature, no physical ecstasy, no suspension of the
faculties. Nor would this lack of the extraordinary indicate that his
experience was less profound than that of the person who lost the
use of his external senses. It would simply mean that he was strong
in body and in psyche. Consequently de Guibert preferred to speak

of three stages: prayer of quiet, union and transforming union; and he looked on ecstasy as no more than an occasional and unimportant by-product of the second stage (Guibert, pt. 7, ch. 2).

De Guibert's theory is probably closer to the truth. Much as I admire and respect Poulain, I think that in this point his scientific bent led him to a false emphasis. Besides, here he sings out of tune with the great chorus of Western mystical thought. It is significant, too, that in Zen, even in the deepest spiritual experiences, physical ecstasy is virtually unknown. If anything like this does rear its head, it is promptly crushed. Indeed, the whole Zen training is calculated to counteract anything like ecstasy. The open eyes keep the meditator in contact with his surroundings; then the scolding and the shouting and the beating with the stick and the general atmosphere of the meditation hall militate against anything like ligature or suspension of the faculties. Dr Suzuki often insisted that Zen was not 'mystical'. I suspect that he disliked this word mysticism precisely because of its association with phenomena like physical ecstasy: the great scholar felt intuitively (and how wisely!) that these bodily things were not what mattered.

Granted all this, however, I still would not reject ecstasy as a stage in mystical development. But I would modify the meaning of the word. I believe that underlying the unimportant physical phenomena is a spiritual experience of the greatest significance which merits our attention. It is an experience that is undoubtedly present also in the deepest stages of Zen: an extraordinarily powerful uprising of spirit in the human mind and heart and the transition to a new level of consciousness. It is this that I call ecstasy (prescinding entirely from ligature and levitation, which may, or may not, be there) and in doing so I believe that I am following a Christian tradition that antedates Poulain and goes back to the thirteenth and fourteenth centuries. For the medieval mystics, ecstasy (the Greek *ekstasis* or *standing out*) was a going out from, or a relinquishing of, the self. This is the root meaning of the term.

Taking it in this sense, I would like to examine more closely this mystical phenomenon and discuss its significance for human life and, more particularly, for human death.

Describing ecstasy, St Teresa speaks of 'a feeling of great joy and sweetness'. 'You realize . . . and indeed see that you are being carried away and know not where. For although this is delightful the

weakness of our nature makes us afraid at first . . . often I should like
to resist . . . especially in a public place' (Teresa (1), ch. 20). From
her accounts, as well as others, we can distinguish two aspects of
ecstasy: joy and fear. There is joy because of the change in consciousness, the inflow or ascendency of spirit, the finding of the new self,
the increase of being. There is fear because of human weakness and
the possible loss of control. One is, so to speak, overwhelmed like a
sinking ship. Yet this fear diminishes as the meditator becomes
capable of controlling the new force that has entered his life. Then
gradually the peak, as already noted, becomes a plateau.

In recent times some psychologists have proposed the hypothesis
that a similar phenomenon takes place at the moment of death.
Studies on sudden death (gathered from people who fell from
mountain-tops or whose parachutes did not open – people who came
to the brink of death yet still lived) have revealed that the dying
person is frequently overwhelmed by what can only be called a
mystical experience resembling ecstasy. This and other studies have
led to the hypothesis that dying persons pass through three psychological stages – resistance, life-review and transcendence. In the first
stage they fight back because, like the ecstatic, they fear the loss of
control. But once they have submitted to the inevitable, memories of
their whole past may arise, all in a flash and in the most minute
detail. Finally comes the mystical consciousness, often described in
terms remarkably like those of the great ecstatics.

No one, of course, claims that everybody dies in ecstasy. The most
that can be said is that ideally speaking this is the way life should end.
And indeed some ancient cultures have felt this way about death.
The task confronting us now is to examine the dispositions and the
attitudes we should cultivate if we are to die in this way. Such knowledge will be of the utmost value and significance. And here St John
of the Cross (who in some ways confirms this psychological hypothesis) comes to the rescue, telling us of one type of person who dies
'with the most sublime impulses and delightful encounters of love'.
This is the mystic. The great Spaniard makes his point quite
clearly:

> The death of such persons is very gentle and very sweet, sweeter
> and more gentle than was their whole spiritual life on earth. For
> they die with the most sublime impulses and delightful encounters
> of love, resembling the swan whose song is much sweeter at the

moment of death. Accordingly, David affirmed that the death of the saints is precious in the sight of the Lord (Psalm 115:15). The soul's riches gather together here, and its rivers of love move on to enter the sea, for these rivers, because they are blocked, become so vast that they themselves resemble seas. The just man's first treasures, and his last, are heaped together to accompany him when he departs and goes off to his kingdom, while praises are heard from the ends of the earth, which, as Isaiah says, are the glory of the just man (Isaiah 24:16).   (John of the Cross, p.592)

Here is a beautiful description of ecstatic death.

Psychological discoveries about ecstasy at death dovetail with modern theological studies about the ageing process. These speak of a double curve in the graph of human life: the downward curve of physical disintegration as the vital forces diminish, and the upward curve of spiritual energies as the core of the personality is liberated.[1] Not, again, that this happens in every case; but ideally speaking it should happen if all goes well. From the earliest times, the Hindus have had the same intuition and they have divided human life into four stages in the course of which the personality is increasingly spiritualized. In the third stage (coming after that of the student and the householder) the now ageing man retires to the forest or to a quiet place to devote himself to the reading of the scriptures and to meditation; while in the final period he embraces the monastic life, rising above all the cares of the world in equanimity and the cultivation of God-consciousness. And then there is Jung, with his thesis that beginning with the middle period of life (thirty-five to forty-five in the West of his day) a person should become increasingly contemplative.

All these theories point to one central idea: that the life of man is (or, more correctly, ought to be) a process of spiritualization which reaches its climax with death. If this is so, what happens abruptly in ecstasy and sudden death may happen gradually in the ageing process. There is the same inflow of spirit, the same expansion of consciousness; but the very slowness of the process makes integration easier. In either case, death is the door to the ultimate ecstasy (call it

[1] See Roger Troisfontaines, *I Do Not Die* (Desclée, New York, 1963); Ladislaus Boros, *The Mystery of Death* (Herder & Herder, New York, 1965), published in Great Britain under the title, *The Moment of Truth: Mysterium Mortis* (Burns & Oates, London, 1965).

resurrection or *nirvana* or what you will), and in the lives of the mystics we find foretastes or adumbrations of this final beatifying ecstasy.

I have constantly spoken about the uprising or transcendence of *spirit*. Now I think the word needs to be explained with more precision. I use it in two senses. First there are the spiritual energies that lie deepest in man, making him cosmic and universal, making him see deeply into reality, making him truly and distinctively human. It is, presumably, about this spirit that Jung and other psychologists speak. But in the Christian tradition, joined to this is another uprising of the Spirit – of the Holy Spirit, of the Spirit of Jesus who cries out, 'Abba! Father!' (Galatians 4:6) This is the Spirit that animated Paul when he exclaimed, 'It is no longer I who live, but Christ who lives in me' (Galatians 2:20). Paul quite surely had both of these meanings in mind when he wrote of the Christian life as a transition from flesh to spirit. We know that the Pauline flesh is not just sensuality, and the Pauline spirit is not the Platonic soul. Rather is the spiritual man the one whose human faculties are highly spiritualized and who acts under the influence of the Spirit. As such, the transition from flesh to spirit represents a movement towards hominization, towards becoming a man fully alive, towards submission to the Spirit of God.

But can we probe a little more into the cause of this ascendency of spirit that we call ecstasy?

Again, I would distinguish. About the uprising of man's spiritual energies we can say something, since this is a psychological phenomenon. But about the rising of the Holy Spirit we can say almost nothing except from theology. For the Spirit is like the wind that breathes where it will. This makes the whole phenomenon drastically charismatic. But about the uprising of the other spiritual energies, I repeat, it should be possible to say something; and, indeed, some psychologists have put forward hypotheses and explanations. Let me, then, refer to one such hypothesis (with which I beg to differ) about the pre-death ecstasy; and then let me tentatively propose my own explanation.

It has been suggested that the ecstasy that precedes sudden death is caused by hopelessness and despair. The future is a blank. Man is faced with inevitable extinction. And so, his vital energies concentrate on the beautiful experiences of the past, which then surge up in a transfigured way. Hence the joy and the ecstasy.

I myself cannot accept a theory which makes ecstasy an emotional reaction against extinction. It does not fit the facts. Even if it accounted for the transfigured life-review, it still would not explain the subsequent mystical experience. Besides, we know that something like ecstasy may take place when people are brought to what psychologists call 'survival level' – even when there is no hopeless prospect of immediate death or extinction. When the body is kicked and beaten and broken and starved and treated as an object, the most profound psychic powers, ordinarily dormant, may be released and something like ecstasy may ensue. But this seems to happen not with the people who have no hope; but on the contrary, in the people who have strong faith and hope and love and motivation. Let me give one striking example.

The story of Viktor Frankl's suffering in concentration camp is well known. Deprived of food and clothing and human comfort of every kind, he had the most beautiful experiences of mystical communion with his deeply loved wife. I cannot believe that this was caused by fear of extinction. He does not indicate that he feared death at all. His account implies that there were two contributing elements: the first was his love, constituting the most powerful motivation, and the second was the total deprivation that he was forced to endure. These two factors opened up a new layer of psychic life that can well be called ecstatic. Frankl himself draws the conclusion that the most important thing for human survival in such circumstances is motivation or faith (hence his logotherapy) but he was also keenly aware of the role of deprivation and detachment in ecstatic experience.

Viktor Frankl's experience is not unique. In the case of the mystics it was precisely when they clung to faith in the most radical detachment that the ecstasy took place. A Buddhist monk once told me that he had his most beautiful interior experiences when he was cold and tired and hungry in time of *sesshin*. I believe that Jesus confirms this when he says that the poor and the persecuted and those that mourn are happy and have their reward. This reward is not just pie in the sky after death; it is a reward here and now. 'Rejoice and be glad, for your reward is great' (Matthew 5:12) As if he were to say, 'If you have faith in me and do not waver, then in suffering and persecution your latent spiritual powers will be brought into play and the truest human joy will well up from the core of your being. So rejoice and

faith in time of suffering and deprivation can release deep latent spiritual powers – joy – psychic life new level of consciousness – Ecstasy be glad with ecstatic joy.' Such is the power of faith; and such is the power of suffering.

Returning to the ecstasy prior to sudden death, then, I would propose that it also is the result of these two elements. On the one hand there is the total deprivation of all that is familiar, the prospect – not of extinction, but of total loss; and the ensuing detachment. And just at this moment, faith wells up in the human heart. In the face of the greatest adversity human faith comes to the fore. Graham Greene speaks somewhere of 'the kind of faith that issues from despair'; and I would hazard the guess that in the person with religious faith the ecstasy is more likely to occur. But in others also, a basic faith in man, a kind of primordial hope that lies deep in all of us – this surges up ecstatically in the human breast. As such I speak of a psychological phenomenon. But from theology we can also say that the action of the Spirit may penetrate this whole process and cry out, 'Abba, Father!'

Asked about the deepest significance of ecstasy, I would say that it is a foretaste of resurrection. It is a step forward in the spiritualization of man; it is a movement to a deeper level of consciousness that is ever more cosmic; it is the death of the old man and the birth of the new. All this reaches its climax, I believe, in resurrection, when man, definitively spiritualized, becomes cosmic in union with Christ who is cosmic and coextensive with all that is. People who have experienced ecstasy have somehow savoured resurrection and that is why they often long for death, like Paul, who wanted to be dissolved and to be with Christ (Philippians 1:23). Having experienced the shadow, he wanted the reality. But only through death is this reality reached. 'Unless a grain of wheat falls into the earth and dies, it remains alone; but if it dies, it bears much fruit' (John 12:24).

Ecstasy is indeed a foreshadowing. It is never the ultimate thing. The pre-death ecstasy is no more than a tiny glimpse, an inkling of what the post-death ecstasy might be. The pre-death ecstasy is still an act of faith: the post-death ecstasy is an act of possession. All the great religious traditions stress that the final consummation is not found in this life. Zen Buddhism says this by its insistence that the meditator never reaches the end. There is always a further step: there is always something beyond: the most sublime states of consciousness are no more than beginnings. How often the self-complacent monk who thinks he has reached the end receives a blow with the salutary reminder that there is no end.

In the Hebrew-Christian tradition, too, it is constantly reiterated that the highest ecstasies and the most profound spiritual raptures are no more than tokens of the final experience of God. They are never the last stage. Moses may meet Yahweh in the cloud of unknowing, but the great prophet never sees Yahweh's face. 'You cannot see my face; for man shall not see me and live' (Exodus 33:20). This is a literary way of saying that consciousness of the absolute is never direct: knowledge of God will never be complete. We can see the rays of the sun: never the sun itself. John of the Cross, humble and patient mystic though he is, gets shrill and angry at the very thought of self-satisfied mystics naïvely believing that their elevated states are the final consummation. To think this is to demean God and to forget that he is beyond anything man's little mind can grasp. The ultimate vision of God is reserved for the resurrection that is attained through death.

So in the last analysis we are left in darkness about the ultimate vision. Ecstasy points to the end. But it is not an end itself. We know very little.

7. *Return to the market-place*

In my last chapter I described the mystical states of consciousness as outlined in Poulain. In Zen a similar attempt to trace the meditational journey is made in the famous Oxherding pictures which depict man in search of the ox – the sacred animal of the East, symbolizing the true self. Successive sketches show man lost in illusion until he gets a glimpse of the footprints of the ox; then of the ox itself. Next he tames the ox and rides it home. Then the ox disappears, leaving the man alone. But the drama reaches its climax with the eighth picture where not only the ox but also the man disappears and nothing remains. Not a thing is. And this is represented by the famous and powerful symbol of nothingness in the form of a circle:

neither man nor ox

八　　　　　　　人牛倶忘

(By kind permission of Kobori Nanrei, Daitokuji, Kyoto)

Thus ended the original set of Oxherding pictures, with the last stage depicting a state of consciousness beyond subject and object in which it is impossible to make a statement or a judgement about anything. This is the undifferentiated or non-discriminating consciousness about which Zen talks so much.

In twelfth-century China, however, other pictures were added, so that the series ended with the enlightened old man returning to the market-place to save all sentient beings:

十　　　　　　入　鄽　垂　手

(By kind permission of Kobori Nanrei, Daitokuji, Kyoto)

These two sketches help us to understand the meditation we are discussing in this book. Such meditation is, ideally speaking, a growth from rationalization to the undifferentiated consciousness represented by the circle, and then on to the loving and compassionate consciousness radiating from the wise old man as he returns to the market-place to save all sentient beings.

rationalization
undifferentiated consciousness.
loving + compassionate consciousness

Let me say a word about each of the pictures.

The undifferentiated consciousness represented by the circle is a fact of experience. No use denying it. As the human mind penetrates more deeply into reality, it becomes increasingly aware of unity. It comes to perceive that everything is one. And, at the same time, it knows that everything is not one. This is the great paradox of mysticism East and West. Experientially, indeed, it is no problem: the person who has delved deeply into reality knows quite simply that everything is one and yet it is not one. But the Greeks (in this point, as in some others, the villains of the piece) were much less open to paradox than their cousins east of Suez; and they built up this problem into the central riddle of all philosophical thinking. They called it *the problem of the one and the many*, and gave it the honoured place in all those philosophical disputations that shook and shaped the Western world. From Parmenides and Heraclitus to Plato, and from Aristotle to Thomas Aquinas the words rang out in syllogistic disputations: 'How can it be that there is only one thing and yet there are many things?'

As I have already said, in the simple experience of the mystic this is a non-problem: the two poles are naturally reconciled. But, like many simple things, it becomes desperately complicated when you begin to theorize about it. While Eastern philosophy scarcely considered the problem, its Hellenistic counterpart set up two opposing and irreconcilable systems, two opposing camps: monism and dualism, pantheism and monotheism.

I do not believe that these systems contradict one another. Rather are they complementary. And this becomes a bit clearer in the thought of less Hellenistic Westerners like Bergson and Whitehead and Teilhard de Chardin. Earlier in this book I have said that it is mainly a question of different states of consciousness: the undifferentiated or non-discriminating consciousness which sees unity, and the differentiated or discriminating consciousness which sees multiplicity. Both of these states are, I believe, valid; and human perfection reaches its climax in a new consciousness where unity and diversity are somehow simultaneously operative in the same person. Just as a person can produce alpha and beta brainwaves at the same time, so he can possess a consciousness that is at the same time discriminating and non-discriminating.

Let me, then, outline three stages of growth to illustrate what I mean.

The first stage is that of the discriminating consciousness where we perceive principally duality. This consciousness is at work in the world of business, science, scholarship. It is a consciousness filled with imagery and thinking, ordinarily producing beta brainwaves. I have already said that Zen, rejecting this consciousness as illusory, works towards the non-discriminating consciousness; whereas the Western mystical tradition values it as a stage in meditational growth, a *path* to the non-discriminating consciousness. Western mysticism has always tried to enter into the intuitive with respect for the rational.

The second stage, represented by the circle, is the undifferentiated consciousness. Here one sees the unity of being. Everything is one. To the person who experiences this oneness in a momentary intuition, it may become difficult to believe again in duality; just as the person without experience of unity can only believe in duality. Perhaps a simple metaphor might help. If I see water, I see one thing. Yet this same water can become two things: hydrogen and oxygen. A simple person might find it difficult to believe that this single liquid can become two gases. Or he might find it equally difficult to believe that the two gases could form a drop of water. Yet we know this is true.

The third stage is found when the above two states become luminous to one another, growing into yet a new consciousness in which there is a total unity and a total alterity, a realization that all is one and yet all is not one. It is to this that Teilhard refers when he claims that union differentiates at the level of the person and that in union with the other I find my true self. This is the experience of the mystic who realizes in a flash of ecstatic love that only God exists and that God is the all – and yet, at the same time, that he himself also exists as a unique person, called by name and loved definitively. 'Abraham, Abraham!' (Genesis 22:11) I doubt if this consciousness can be experienced apart from ecstatic love encounter. Yet it perdures in what I have called the transforming union. Like the first consciousness it can be at work in business, science and scholarship. For the wheel has turned a full circle. The wise old man has returned to the market-place.

Let me make a few more comments on these stages of consciousness in relation to the mysticism of the West.

First of all, it seems to me that the Western insight about developing both the discriminating and non-discriminating dimension in man is valuable. The balanced and integral human person needs both rational and intuitive power. This, it seems, can even be shown biologically from recent research on the human brain. It has become clear that each of the two giant hemispheres which, joined by the *corpus callosum*, go to make up the human brain, has a distinctive role. The left hemisphere deals with words and thinking and reasoning and what are called verbal skills, in such wise that a lesion in this hemisphere will cause one to forget the words of a song even when one remembers the melody. The right hemisphere, on the other hand, is concerned with music, art, contemplation, silent meditation, in such wise that a lesion here will cause one to forget the melody of a song even when one remembers the words. Some scientists working in the Langley Porter Institute in San Francisco begin to talk about a *left-hemisphere culture* and a *right-hemisphere culture* (Segal, p. 328). The former is rationalistic, philosophical, technological – the kind of culture that has predominated for the past few centuries in the West. The right-hemisphere culture, on the other hand, is artistic and contemplative – I would say that in spite of its tremendous technological advances Japan's culture is still predominantly right-hemisphere.

The point I wish to make here, however, is that for human perfection both hemispheres should be developed. Otherwise man remains one-sided and unbalanced.

I have always believed that respect for rationality is something that Zen can learn from dialogue with the West. The great Zen philosopher Nishida Kitaro seems to have seen this. Rooted in Zen, he was also steeped in Western philosophy. Perhaps he was looking for a rational system that would balance and strengthen the silent intuitiveness of Zen.

The Judaeo-Christian tradition has always made much of the dualistic element since its notion of prayer centres around a relationship of love between two free agents. 'You shall love the Lord your God with all your heart . . .' (Deuteronomy 6:4). But the first, purely discriminating consciousness is no more than a stage towards the third experience of unity and diversity.

This third stage stands out gloriously in the seventeenth chapter of the fourth gospel where Jesus prays that his disciples may be one, that they may be perfectly one, that they may be completely one –

unity in duality

'even as thou, Father, art in me, and I in thee'. And yet they are not
one; because each retains his own personality.

Something similar is found in St Paul. His first encounter with
Christ on the road to Damascus takes the form of a dialogue: 'Who
are you, Lord?' (Acts 9:5) But in the later epistles a new dialogue
appears. For now Paul is 'in Christ' and the Spirit of Jesus within is
calling out, 'Abba! Father!' (Galatians 4:6) So we find enacted within
Paul a dialogue between the Father and the Son, who are perfectly
one yet remain distinct. As for Paul himself, he can claim that his
very life is the life of the Son of God who loved him and gave himself
up for him (Galatians 2:20); and Christ is 'the fullness of him who
fills all' (Ephesians 1:23). Paul has died and his life lies hidden with
Christ in God (Colossians 3:3). What *koan* Paul used! And they can
be understood only in the light of a consciousness in which everything is one, and yet it is not one.

Before going on to discuss the second picture let me quote two
more examples of these stages of consciousness. The first is from
Zen. I was greatly impressed when I heard a master say that after
attending to the breathing for some time, one realizes that there are
two distinct stages in Zen. One is:

I am breathing.

The next is:

The universe is breathing.

This is a fine example of the undifferentiated consciousness and the
loss of self.

My second example is from St John of the Cross, and it also deals
with breathing and awakening. It is at the end of his exquisite little
poem *The Living Flame*, where he comes to write about the great
enlightenment:

How gently and lovingly thou awakest in my bosom, where thou
dwellest secretly and alone!
And in thy sweet breathing, full of blessing and glory, how
delicately thou inspirest my love!

Note that he does not say *I* am enlightened, or *I* awaken – because this *I* is gone. Rather does he say (and he explains himself more at length in his commentary) that *the Word awakens in me*. This has something in common with the universe awakening and breathing; except that the Word inspires his love, and this is the love of the Son for the Father. Here again we have a wonderful example of that consciousness in which all is one and yet all is not one.

The second sketch depicts the return to the market-place. The charming, enlightened old sage, having entered the supreme consciousness of unity and duality, returns to save all sentient beings. That there is indeed an element of duality here can scarcely be denied. If the kind old man returns to save all sentient beings, then must there not be sentient beings to save?

Though the final picture is a twelfth-century appendage, it nevertheless forms a fitting and beautiful climax to the Zen journey, in which presence to reality and incarnationalism have always been stressed and are now doubly stressed with the additional dimension of exquisite Buddhist compassion, the highest form of activity.

Here is a typical passage from a Zen master who asserts that the deepest enlightenment is found by hurling oneself into the maelstrom of activity:

> The superior work you have done so industriously in quietness should be applied when you are submerged in the tumult of your daily life. If you find it difficult to do so, it is most likely that you have not gained much from the work of quietude. If you are convinced that meditating in quietude is better than meditating in activity, you are then [falling into the trap of] searching for reality through destroying manifestations, or of departing from causation to pursue Nirvana. *The very moment when you are craving quiet and abhorring turbulence is the best time to put all your strength into the work. Suddenly the realization which you have searched so hard for in your quiet meditation will break upon you right in the midst of turbulence.* Oh, this power, gained from breaking-through, is thousands and millions of times greater than that generated by quiet meditation on your straw seat and bamboo chair.   (Chang, p. 88)

As far as practical advice is concerned, the above might well have been written by the soldier-saint, Ignatius of Loyola. He also wanted to hurl people into the turbulence of action, there to experience the divine and to find enlightenment. Nor in this was he a revolutionary innovator. Through the centuries Western mysticism waged a constant and relentless battle against Gnosticism, Neoplatonism and flight from matter. Though the states of consciousness outlined by Poulain may at first look escapist, the opposite is in fact true. No one insists on incarnationalism more than St Teresa. For her the mystic must have both feet planted firmly on the ground, must never let himself be divorced from reality.

Here are some typical sentences from *The Interior Castle*:

> Oh, my sisters, how little we should think about resting . . . For if the soul is much with him . . . it will seldom think of itself. Its whole thought will be concentrated on finding ways to please him and upon showing him how it loves him. *This . . . is the aim of prayer; this is the purpose of the Spiritual Marriage of which are born good works and good works alone.*
>
> (Teresa (2), Seventh Mansion, ch. 4)

And in the same chapter she continues:

> You may think that I am speaking about beginners and that later on you may rest; but as I have told you, the only repose that these souls enjoy is of an interior kind; *of outward repose they get less and less and have no wish to get more.*

And again:

> We should desire and engage in prayer not for our enjoyment but for the sake of acquiring this strength which fits us for service.

It should be noted that this stress on active service appears in Teresa's seventh mansion, which is the very pinnacle of the mystical life. In this respect it parallels the return to the market-place which comes at the end of the Zen journey.

But how keep in touch with reality? How keep one's feet on the ground in such a lofty business as meditation? In Zen this is done by a series of techniques such as a deliberate policy of keeping the eyes open, of never closing the doors of the senses, of always remaining close to the environment, and so on. For Teresa, however, incarnationalism is ensured by never abandoning the humanity of Christ, even in the loftiest flights of contemplation. If any one point is stressed and stressed again in the saint of Avila it is the centrality of the humanity of Christ. To this she constantly returns as the main norm for judging the authenticity of Christian meditation. And she claims that meditation rooted in the humanity of Christ will avoid the danger of airy-fairy floating in inner space.

However, it is very important to discover what Teresa means by *the humanity of Christ*. One thing is clear: she by no means insists that the meditator entertain thoughts and concepts of the historical Jesus as he lived in Nazareth or in Galilee. Rather is she concerned with the universal Christ – who is, of course, the same Jesus since there is only one Christ. But now he is seen in his risen existence. In her *Life* she writes:

> Withdrawal from bodily objects must no doubt be good since it is recommended by spiritual persons . . . But what I should like to make clear is that *Christ's humanity must not be reckoned among these bodily objects. This must be clearly understood and I wish I knew how to explain it.*   (Teresa (1), ch. 22)

And again in *The Interior Castle*:

> This secret union [the spiritual marriage] takes place in the deepest centre of the soul which must be where God himself dwells and I do not think there is need of a door by which to enter it . . . all that has been described seems to have come through the medium of the senses and faculties and this appearance of the humanity of the Lord must do so too. *But what passes in the union of the spiritual marriage is very different. The Lord appears in the centre of the soul . . . just as he appeared to the Apostles, without entering through the door, when he said to them 'Pax Vobis'* . . . he [St Paul] . . . says, 'For me to live is Christ and to die is gain.' This, I think, the soul may say here . . . because Christ is now its life.
>   (Teresa (2), Seventh Mansion, ch. 11)

Remember that the above words are written about the very summit of contemplation. There is no question here of the discursive, imageful prayer of beginners but of the highest stages of mysticism.

the Cosmic Jesus

And Christ is there. He is not, she says explicitly, the 'bodily' Christ, even though he is quite surely the same person as the historical Jesus. In short, Teresa is quite certain that Christ is present, that it is not the 'bodily' Christ, and that she simply does not have concepts to express Christ as he is ('I wish I knew how to explain it'). That it is the risen Christ (and therefore the cosmic Christ) is amply clear from the whole context which speaks of the Lord who appeared to the disciples and passed through doors – the Lord with whom Paul identifies his very life.

I myself believe that she means what Teilhard calls the cosmic Christ, a reality beyond images and concepts, fully compatible with the highest stages of imageless, nonconceptual prayer. I am not saying that Teresa talks explicitly about the cosmic Christ; but that she was striving for words to express something that centuries later was formulated by Teilhard in this way.

Let me speak briefly about the background to Teilhard's doctrine of the cosmic Christ.

Reading the New Testament quite simply, the chief point that stands out in the whole text is that Jesus who died is now alive. He is among us and will be with us all days even to the consummation of the world. In what shape or form he exists among us is not clearly said; and St Paul, when asked about the nature of the risen body, simply answers, 'Don't ask foolish questions!' ('But some one will ask, "How are the dead raised? With what kind of body do they come?" You foolish man! . . .' (1 Corinthians 15:35).) So about the nature of the resurrected body, either of Christ or of anyone else, we can say little. Only two things are clear from the New Testament. On the one hand, it is the same Jesus as before, still retaining his wounds. On the other hand, it is a transformed Jesus – so much so that his intimate friends do not recognize him for some time.

Of the many interpretations of this phenomenon of the risen Christ I myself incline to the Teilhardian which I regard as a valid development of St Paul's and which, I believe, is somehow present in St Teresa. In death, says Teilhard, Christ becomes cosmic and is present among us as the Christ of the universe, who now possesses a new relationship to matter. He is physically present (and in this sense he is 'bodily') but with a new kind of matter. Teilhard uses words like 'hyperphysics', but he is trying to express the inexpressible.

All this may sound a bit complicated and abstruse, but it is of the

utmost importance for the Christian who wishes to make his meditation Christocentric while retaining the imageless silence of
contemplation. Without in any way downgrading the meditation
that reflects on the words and life of the historical Jesus of Nazareth,
it can safely be said that this is not the kind of meditation Teresa of
Avila teaches in the deeper mansions. When she insists on the
centrality of Christ, she is talking about the cosmic Christ who is
coextensive with the universe and of whom no adequate picture can
be formed. This is indeed the Christ who appears all through the
fourth gospel saying, 'I am the true vine; I am the true shepherd; I
am the true bread; I am the way', and so on. 'I, when I am lifted up
from the earth, will draw all men to myself' (John 12:32). By his
resurrection he is the reality in which every other reality exists.

Once we grasp this, we see that the Christian must perforce
remain with the risen Jesus just as the Buddhist cannot escape the
Buddha nature. But this does not mean that he *thinks constantly
about* Christ any more than the Buddhist thinks constantly about the
Buddha nature. Rather will he turn to the Father whom Christ has
revealed and to whom Christ points. That is why when one has put
on the mind of Christ there comes a time when, in a true sense, only
the Father remains. But both feet will be firmly on the ground.
Because the Christian believes that the risen Christ is the deepest
reality (just as the Buddhist believes something similar about the
Buddha nature) and that by remaining with Christ he remains close
to the heart of the universe.

Finally let me say that we should not take this return to the market-
place in a too literal or too simplistic way. In a sense, the dichotomy
between contemplation and action is a false statement of the problem.
Since contemplation is activity – the highest form of activity – it is in
itself a return to the market-place and a building of the earth. This
is clear in Teilhard, who, among the many ways of forwarding the
thrust of an ongoing evolution, regards mysticism as the most effective
and the most powerful. This is because in mysticism the very highest
form of human energy is brought into play, a human energy that is
nothing other than love at the core of one's being. It is precisely this
that builds the earth. Zen hints at this when it claims that the Zen
master 'sits' for the whole universe. And *The Cloud of Unknowing*
speaks of it, too, when it declares that this little love is helping all
mankind and giving joy to the hearts of the dead. Here a whole

mysticism = highest form of energy
because it is the energy of love

cosmic energy is unleashed and the world shakes. More things are wrought by prayer than this world dreams of.

Writers like John of the Cross tell us that one act of pure love achieves more than all the exterior works in the whole world. And, of course, we have tended to dismiss all this as pious hyperbole. But now some scientists are beginning to say things like that. Some scientists are open to the hypothesis that in meditation a life-force is released which is more significant than nuclear energy. The energy that science looks to is not, of course, the whole story. Bioplasmic energy and passive energy (about which I shall speak in a later chapter) may be a basis for the even higher energy of faith and love that no instrument can measure.

So contemplation and action may not be opposed. One will often return to the market-place while remaining on one's meditation cushion or at the prie-dieu. The return to the market-place need not be a further step. It is part of the very activity of meditation.

8. *A perilous journey*

If travel in outer space is fraught with danger, in such wise that we need intrepid astronauts, even more perilous is the inner journey into the caverns of the mind. The astronaut might lose his life: the inner explorer might lose even more precious things. This point was made by a group of scientists whose words, quoted in an earlier chapter, might bear repetition here. 'These inner forces are very powerful', they wrote. 'Beware the dangers that exist when work like this is done, especially by large numbers of people, without the high values and lifelong discipline of the great ancient systems' (Weide, p. 84). Clearly these scientists are aware that religious people, rooted in the great spiritual systems, are less likely to have a bad trip than the psychologist or the layman.

The reason for this, I would suggest, is not only the high values and lifelong discipline of the great ancient systems. Other forces are at work. There is the action of ultimate reality moving towards man (action which we call grace), and together with this there is the extremely powerful and unifying motivation that underlies the journey of the mystic searching for that which he loves. 'Seeking my beloved, I will go over the mountains', writes St John of the Cross. 'I will pluck no flowers, I will fear no wild beasts.' As if to say that even if all kinds of seductive images and frightening beasts rise up from the womb of the unconscious, he will pay no attention to them because he has heard the even more seductive call of his beloved – who is 'the mountains, the solitary wooded valleys, strange islands . . . silent music'. This depth of faith and singleness of purpose make his trip infinitely safer than that of the person who begins to roam around in the caverns of his own mind. Such a person might easily get lost.

But before going on, let me digress for a moment to make clear my distinction between the mystic and the explorer in consciousness. This is important because I believe that some modern people think they are practising religion when in fact they are exploring their inner world. The world of the mystic and the world of the psychic explorer, it is true, have much in common and they overlap. Both are inner mansions of hypnagogic imagery, unconscious locution, exquisite symbolism and violent upheaval. But whereas the interest of the psychic researcher lies in this world itself, the mystic is passionately in love with a reality that lies beyond consciousness. His main interest is in something or someone he loves but can never fully grasp. For him expansion of mind and states of consciousness are unimportant consequences of his great love.

Yet the dividing line is fine. Jung and Huxley, primarily psychic explorers, were also deeply religious men. And Poulain, primarily a theologian, was also an acute psychological researcher. So their terrains overlap.

Here, first of all, I would like to select two psychological dangers or snares that confront both the psychic explorer and the mystic. The first is flight from reality, withdrawal into one's own world: the escape syndrome. The second is a too rapid or premature entry into higher states of consciousness. When either of these things happens, a person may find himself unable to control and integrate the images and the knowledge that suddenly flood his psyche. Let me illustrate this with an example that may be of interest.

In a study of mysticism and schizophrenia, Kenneth Wapnick compares St Teresa of Avila with an anonymous schizophrenic who left a diary containing detailed descriptions of her inner life. In the experiences of these two persons Wapnick discovers certain parallels such as the working of a similar psychological mechanism. But he finds more differences. Chief among these is the fact that the schizophrenic, totally unadjusted to ordinary life, retreated into her own world whereas St Teresa kept integrating her inner experiences with daily living. She led a happy life in community with other people and succeeded in doing an enormous amount of work. Wapnick considers this (which, in fact, is Teresa's return to the market-place) to be of the greatest significance. He indicates that in both cases many of the psychic experiences have a similar ring, but their adaptation to life is radically different; and he concludes that 'the mystic provides the example of the method whereby the inner and the outer world may be joined, the schizophrenic the tragic result when they are separated' (Wapnick, p. 66).

In the same article, Wapnick goes on to elaborate the distinction between the mystic and the schizophrenic. In the latter, he says, a protective shell is suddenly and prematurely broken, whereas the mystic goes to the depth of his being in gradual stages and in a controlled way. Consequently there is an organic growth in the psychic life of the mystic, who becomes more and more a person. Wapnick quotes Jung, who, at a time when he was exploring the deepest levels of the psyche, felt the need of family life and professional work to keep him in touch with reality, to reassure him that he was after all an ordinary person, and to preserve him from a too sudden exposure to his own inner world. Like Teresa he had to keep integrating the emerging data of consciousness into daily living, and without this he might well have become psychotic. We know that drug addicts often break down because they cannot cope with the images released by the ingestion of drugs. Therapy, then, consists in helping them integrate these images.

All this perhaps confirms the age-old Western teaching that the best norm for distinguishing the mystic from the neurotic is daily life. The great masters put less store on what was happening in the mind during prayer than upon the person's life outside prayer. No doubt St Teresa would have asked few questions about a mystic's scores on the EEG even if she had known all about the psychophysiology of contemplation. Rather would she have asked about his adaptability to community living, his humble service to others, his habits of hard work, his ability to do drudgery. It was by these common-or-garden norms that she, and others like her, judged the quality of mysticism. Above all, she put great store on the person's ability to submit to truth; and she kept saying, 'Humility, humility, humility!', as if to say that the ego vanishes when the experience is real.

Because of the great perils involved, most religious traditions have sought to initiate their devotees into mystical silence rather than allowed them to wander freely into the deeper caverns of the mind. This is done in various ways. In Zen, for example, the master will tell the disciple when the time has come to give up breath-counting and enter into deep and imageless silence. Or he will give him the *koan* which he thinks will help him. In Western Christianity direction was considered important (though less important than in most Eastern systems), but it was supplemented by certain signs for discerning the right time for entrance into the subliminal depths of contemplation. These signs, however, were more than psychological norms for judging the aptitude of an aspirant to mysticism. They were ways for judging the action of the Spirit. For the whole Christian tradition

God must call us first!

asserts that Christian contemplative prayer is a response to a divine call ('Let us love God "because he first loved us" ' (1 John 4:19)) and that one should not enter hastily into the interior mansions lest one anticipate the invitation of the Spirit. 'Stir not up nor awaken love until it please' (Song of Solomon 2:7) was a scriptural text constantly used to warn the would-be mystic that only the Spirit can awaken his contemplative love. Here let me summarize these traditional signs.[1]

The first sign was that the person aspiring to contemplation should have undergone a conversion and be totally dedicated to good. It is obvious why this stipulation was made. All the religious traditions know of a mysticism of evil. I remember being shocked when I first heard of a '*samadhi* of pure evil'. I thought of Shakespeare's Iago and the cold-blooded mystical hatred with which he calmly plotted the overthrow of his noble friend Othello. No doubt he would have

① *Conversion*

[1] My sources for these signs are principally *The Cloud of Unknowing*, *The Book of Privy Counselling*, and St John of the Cross. All do not have the same number of signs or exactly the same descriptions, but they are remarkably similar in what they point to.

The Ascent of Mount Carmel, 11, 13 gives signs for discontinuing discursive meditation: (1) Inability to receive satisfaction as before. (2) Disinclination to fix one's attention on things extraneous to prayer. (3) Attraction to solitude in order to remain in loving awareness of God. (4) That all three are present together.

The Dark Night, 1, 9 gives signs indicating that one's aridity in meditation is the beginning of the night of sense: (1) Absence of sense of satisfaction from things of sense or spirit. (2) Memory turns towards God in painful anxiety lest it may not be pleasing him. (3) Inability to meditate as before.

The Minor Works: Maxims and Counsels, 40. There are three signs of inner recollection: first, a lack of satisfaction in passing things; second, a liking for solitude and silence and an attentiveness to all that is more perfect; third, the considerations, meditations and acts which formerly helped the soul now hinder it and it brings to prayer no other support than faith, hope and love.

The Cloud of Unknowing, ch. 75: (1) Purified conscience. (2) Strong attraction to contemplation. (3) Desire for it when it seems to be absent.

The Book of Privy Counselling: (1) Meditation becomes impossible because of the intrusion of contemplation. (2) Increasing joyful attraction for contemplation. (3) The presence of both together.

Good summary of the signs that one is moving into contemplation

produced high-amplitude alpha on the EEG; but it would have been an alpha of evil. It was to obviate such enormities that tradition asked for a conversion prior to entry into the contemplative path. The person with mystical gifts must not use them for destructive ends. If he does, God help us all!

The second traditional sign was the desire for solitude and the longing to be alone. 'How dearly you will love to sit apart by yourself,' writes *The Book of Privy Counselling*, 'knowing that others who did not share your desire and attraction, could only hinder you. Gone will be all your desire to read or to hear books, for your only desire will be to hear of it' (Johnston (1), ch. 19). The 'it' is the contemplative urge, the action of the Spirit which the same author calls 'the blind stirring of love'. This is all important. The desire of solitude itself could be neurotic (indication of 'bad humours', says St John of the Cross) unless it is accompanied by a longing for the infinite.

The third sign was the inability to think discursively in time of meditation – or, at least, a disinclination to do so. At the beginning of the spiritual odyssey one has, perhaps, reflected on the Bible and prayed with psalms and colloquies. But now one is, as it were, held in the grip of something deeper which impedes thought; and one takes no satisfaction in pious reflections as before. Perhaps this is because the first stage in the development of human consciousness (the rational stage) has been gone through and one is ready for the intuitive: the left hemisphere of the brain has done its work and the time has come for further development of the right hemisphere. Unable to think discursively, one rests in silence. It is a situation like that of two people in love, who prefer to sit silently side by side because thinking and talking would only dissipate their loving union. They are not idling: they are united by a bond that needs neither word nor thought. And it is the same with the person who is beginning to commune with the inner flame of love.

The fourth sign is the constant presence of the contemplative urge. This interior movement at a subliminal depth begins to guide and to dominate in one's life. It has been variously called 'the living flame of love', 'the dark night', 'the blind stirring of love', 'the naked intent of the will'. *The Book of Privy Counselling* says well that all that is said is 'about it' but not 'it'. This author insists that such an interior motion of love must always be with the contemplative. If it is only present sometimes, then one cannot be sure that the contemplative call is real. 'So abounding will it be, that it will follow you to bed at night and rise with you in the morning. It will pursue you through the day in everything you do, intruding into your usual daily devotions like a barrier between you and them . . .' (Johnston (1), ch. 19).

St John of the Cross and the author of *The Cloud* insist that all these signs be present at the same time. The presence of only one is no proof of the contemplative call. But all together indicate the action of the Spirit and not just a psychological state symptomatic of neurosis.

I have spoken about the psychological dangers lurking in the path of one who would enter deeply into the interior castle. But there are perils of another kind, more spiritual and peculiarly mystical. Chief among these is the danger of being seduced by the sirens of bewitching beauty that one encounters on the way. For there may be delectable experiences – voices and visions and profusions of joy. Or there may be a serene and restful silence that inundates one's whole being and fills it with peace. Or it may be the siren of discursive thought and reasoning that beguiles – beautiful thoughts about God and his angels and saints. Thinking, as I have repeatedly pointed out, has its part to play in the mystical life; but there is a stage in which it can be a snare. In fact all these experiences, good and holy in themselves, are snares in the mystical life when one makes them an end or seeks them for themselves. They are snares if one clings to them as if they were absolutes: because then one sticks there, stagnates, makes no progress. One must go on and on, clinging to nothing, absolutely nothing, in order to be free and attentive to the living flame of love that burns quietly and wounds the soul in its deepest centre. Yet there is another temptation even more subtle than this.

It is well known that with growth in mysticism comes growth in human potential – greater insight, refined perception, intuitive power and even extrasensory perception. In all the great religious traditions, these powers, known in Sanskrit as *siddhis* are a by-product of the true mystical experience and must never be sought for themselves. They can be a snare, a dangerous fascination distracting the mystic from his true goal which is wisdom in emptiness, the all which is nothing. In early Buddhism, misuse of psychic powers for self-glorification was one of the sins which merited expulsion from the monastery. That is why researchers and experimenters who want subjects to demonstrate such powers in the laboratory may have a hard task in finding cooperative monks. It is not, I repeat, that these powers are evil in themselves. On the contrary, they are good and can be used to help and to heal, as we see done in the New Testament; but like money, which is also good but difficult to use well, they can be a temptation. Clinging to them blinds insight and hinders progress.

That they can be a tremendous temptation must be clear to anyone. If all power fascinates and corrupts, how much more fascinating and corrupting is the lure of psychic power over the minds of other men! This is a terrible temptation: Dr Faustus, selling his soul to the Devil for psychic power, is a truly archetypal figure. Who would not be tempted to a deal with Mephistopheles with the promise of controlling the minds and the actions of other men? Undoubtedly this is one of the great temptations of those who go the whole way in mysticism. Can one not even find a hint of it in the temptations of Jesus? 'The devil took him up, and showed him all the kingdoms of the world in a moment of time, and said to him, "To you I will give all this authority and their glory; for it has been delivered to me, and I give it to whom I will. If you, then, will worship me, it shall all be yours" ' (Luke 4:5–7). What a mystical experience this was, seeing 'in a moment of time' the totality of things! And then the temptation to power!

Of course our outlook on all this will depend to some extent on our interpretation of the Faust motif – whether we interpret Mephistopheles as a really transcendently existing evil or as a projection of the mind of Faust. Are the witches in Macbeth or the ghost in Hamlet or the evil spirits and Satan and the rest – are these real entities or are they no more than projections of the interior ambition and fear and anger and hatred that lurk in the heart of man?

On this point I would like once again to quote Dr Elmer Green of the Menninger Foundation in Kansas. He is treating of precisely the subject that occupies us here; namely, the dangers of a hasty descent into the deeper realms of the mind. After speaking about illusion and hallucination, he goes on:

According to various warnings, the persistent explorer in these . . . realms . . . *brings himself to the attention of indigenous beings who, under normal circumstances, pay little attention to humans . . .* Systems for inner exploration describe these indigenous beings as entities whose bodies are composed entirely of emotional, mental, and etheric substance, and say that at this level of development they are psychologically no better than average man himself. They are of many natures and some are malicious, cruel and cunning, and use the emergence of the explorer out of his previously protective cocoon with its built-in barriers of mental and emotional substance as an opportunity to move, in reverse so to speak, into the personal subjective realm of the investigator.. If he is not relatively free from personality dross, it is said, they can obsess him with various compulsions for their own amusement and in extreme cases can even disrupt the normally automatic functioning of the nervous system, by controlling the brain through the *chakras*. Many mental patients have made the claim of being controlled by subjective entities, *but the doctors in general regard these statements as part of the behavioral aberration, pure subconscious projections, and do not investigate further.*   (Green (4))

The above surprised me a little. Not because of its contents (which are fairly orthodox in any religious tradition) but because it comes from the pen or the typewriter of one of the leading neuropsychiatrists in the US, who also worked for fifteen years as a physicist on rocket and guided missile research. It is one more example of the interdisciplinary approach. A scientist extrapolates into the field of religion. I reflected that a decade ago religious people were affirming the existence of devils, while the scientist smiled with amused incredulity. But now, just as we find religious people doubting about devils, we find scientists affirming their existence. And so the wheel turns.

For Dr Green, then, a great peril in this inner journey is the confrontation with these indigenous beings. Interesting too is his suggestion that they may influence the brain through the *chakras*. These latter are centres of psychic energy that play an important role in Yoga; and the notion that indigenous entities act on them parallels the traditional Christian teaching that the evil spirit takes his stand at the gateway between sense and spirit, making his impact not at the deepest point of the spirit but upon the imagination. If only one could get beyond sense to the core of one's being, said the old doctrine, one had nothing to fear from the evil spirit. 'Have no fear of the evil one for he will not dare come near you. Be he ever so cunning he is powerless to violate the inner sanctum of your will, although he will sometimes attempt it by indirect means. Even an angel cannot touch your will directly. God alone may enter here' (Johnston (1), ch. 34). The suggestion of Dr Green that this impact is made on the *chakras* is an interesting physiological addition to the traditional doctrine.

About these indigenous beings not much can be said. Perhaps it is enough here to recall that orthodox Christianity has never accepted the notion of a Manichaean principle of evil. If beings are evil this is because, originally good, they chose to be evil. They were not created so; and their destructive power is limited and restricted.

All this brings us to the problem of false mysticism. The great religions are at one in affirming the existence of a mysticism that is true and a mysticism that is false. For modern people, it must be admitted, the terminology is none too attractive. How can an experience be 'false'? Psychologists speak of states of consciousness that are *adaptive* or beneficial and *maladaptive* or harmful. But false mysticism says more than this. In general it means that certain states of consciousness are undesirable because they are irrelevant or morbid or regressive, or because they lead away from reality and wisdom, or because they lead to evil or to self-glorification or to destruction or to hatred. All of which are real possibilities. The term 'false mysticism' is taken from the Western mystical tradition. Buddhism speaks of *miccha samadhi* (Pali) or *mithya samadhi* (Sanskrit), literally 'left-handed contemplation', meaning that one gets one-pointed about the wrong things. Certainly, call it what you will, the phenomenon of mystical aberration is well-known in the history of any evolving religion. Nor is discernment easy, because one seldom, if ever, finds mysticism that is one-hundred-per-cent 'true'. Even in the greatest mystics one finds elements of self-deception or illusion as well as emotional disturbances and the ordinary mental sickness to which mortal man is heir.

In the West, ability to distinguish between true and false mysticism, as between true and false prophets, was called discernment. This was a charismatic gift of the Spirit, given to certain people for building up the community (1 Corinthians 12:7). The person with discernment could judge intuitively. Having the Spirit himself, he could recognize the action of the Spirit in others while being sensitive to the action of less desirable spirits too. Stories are told of how great masters like St John of the Cross, hearing of the ecstatic prayer of

certain mystics, would sniff the air of the convent and state con-
fidently, 'No, no! This is not it!' Something a little similar (though
not quite the same) is found in Zen where the master often judges in
a flash that the disciple is enlightened. Sometimes, it is said, he can
judge from the very face of the disciple before a word is spoken. Or
even from the sound of the disciple's footsteps on the corridor
outside.

Unlike Zen, however, Christian mysticism has always insisted
that any intuitive judgement should be backed up by a rational
check. This is in keeping with a whole frame of mind (to which I
have referred several times) which always respects the rational while
going beyond it. And the norms for discernment were summed up
in certain formulae which came to be known as 'rules for the
discernment of spirits'.

These rules have their roots in the New Testament. 'Beloved, do
not believe every spirit, but test the spirits to see whether they are of
God; for many false prophets have gone out into the world' (1 John
4:1). So we are to test the spirits; and for Christian prayer the New
Testament gives a clearcut norm: 'By this you know the Spirit of
God: every spirit which confesses that Jesus Christ has come in the
flesh is of God, and every spirit which does not confess Jesus is not
of God' (1 John 4:2). In other words, the norm is Christ: if a person's
meditation leads him to deeper faith and commitment to Jesus Christ
who came in the flesh, then it is true; if not, it is false. Meditation
should somehow culminate in the act of faith: 'Jesus is Lord!'
(1 Corinthians 12:3)

Obviously this norm is only for Christians, but it may not be
without value for others also. Because underlying it is a stress on
incarnationalism that is of interest for any kind of meditation –
the keeping in touch with reality, the keeping one's feet on the
ground that I have spoken about in reference to St Teresa. John's
words seem to have been written at a time when dualistic Gnosticism
and flight from matter were rife in the Mediterranean world. Hence
his emphasis on the flesh and blood of Jesus. 'That which was from
the beginning, which we have heard, which we have seen with our
eyes, which we have looked upon and touched with our hands . . .'
(1 John 1:1).

Following on this, the acid test of meditation in the New Testament is its fruits. 'But the fruit of the Spirit is love, joy, peace,
patience, kindness, goodness, faithfulness, gentleness, self-control;

against such there is no law' (Galations 5:22). To judge the validity
of interior motions and inspirations is not easy; but the effects or the
fruits are more apparent. Among these, it is interesting to see how
the whole Christian tradition stressed the great significance of peace.
Non in commotione dominus ran the old Latin tag – 'The Lord is not
in commotion'. And spiritual masters like Ignatius of Loyola give
detailed norms for distinguishing between true and false peace. And
again they always asked about the fruits of this peace.

It is scarcely possible here to enter into detail about these rules.
Only let me refer in conclusion to an important one: people who
meditate were always counselled to open their hearts to a director,
particularly in time of stress and temptation. Here is the quaint
advice of St Ignatius:

> The enemy also acts like a false lover who wishes to be hidden and
> does not want to be known. For when this deceitful man pays
> court, with evil intention, to the daughter of some good man or the
> wife of a good husband, he wants his words and suggestions to be
> kept secret. He is greatly upset if the girl tells her father, or the
> wife her husband, his deceitful words and depraved intentions,
> for he sees clearly that then his plans will fail. In the same way,
> when the enemy of our human nature tempts a just soul with his
> tricks and deceits, he wants and desires that they be received and
> kept secret. When they are revealed to a confessor or some other
> spiritual person who understands his deceits and evil designs, the
> enemy is greatly displeased for he knows that he cannot win in his
> evil plan once his obvious deceits have been laid bare.
>
> (Ignatius, p. 132)

The above has something in common with our modern counselling. Except that its aim is to discern the Spirit. Once again it is part
of a whole incarnational thrust in Christian meditation. Any inspiration or enlightenment or action of the Spirit is not complete until it
is manifested to another and thus 'incarnated'. How clear this was
in the case of Paul! His great enlightenment on the road to Damascus
was not complete until manifested to Ananias. With the imposition
of those hands, the scales fell from Paul's eyes and he sat down to eat
and drink. His enlightenment was now complete (Acts 9:18).

I have written a lot about the perilous journey. My intention is not to make people scared. 'Pay no heed to anyone who tries to frighten you or depicts to you the perils of the way', writes Teresa. 'What a strange idea that one could ever expect to travel a road infested by thieves for the purpose of gaining some great treasure without running into danger!' (Teresa (3), ch. 21) The treasure is the thing. And it is worth any effort and risk. But the thieves are there too, and it would be unrealistic to overlook them in one's journey towards wisdom.

PART III

HEALING

9. *Meditation, therapy and passive energy*

Recent times have seen a good deal of interest in meditation as therapy. Western medicine, it is now recognized, has been desperately one-sided, largely ignoring the role of the mind in the healing of the human body. Assuredly it is acknowledged that up to eighty per cent of modern sickness is either psychosomatic in origin or has a psychosomatic dimension (in particular, diseases which are peculiarly human and do not afflict animals are now regarded as psychosomatic); but while admitting psychosomatic sickness, the West has been slow in developing a process of psychosomatic health – that is to say, health of body that will stem from health of mind or from mental control of bodily functions. Only now with the growing influence of the East and talk about acupuncture, about the life-force, about *kundalini* and the rest – only now do we begin to grasp again the spiritual and metaphysical dimensions of healing. But interest is growing fast. And it is not unlikely that meditation will be one of the principal means of therapy in the future.

That meditation has strange and profound repercussions on bodily functions was recognized long ago by the British in India. While Rudyard Kipling sang blithely about the glories of the Empire, more penetrating and common-sensical British medical minds were examining stories about holy men, yogis, who reportedly walked on live coals, had themselves buried alive, stopped their hearts, listened during sleep, pierced their flesh with bloodless swords and defied the laws of gravity. What was the medical profession to think of all that? Was it fact or fiction or myth?

One of the first scientific studies on these phenomena was made by a French cardiologist, Thérèse Brosse, who went to India in 1935 with a portable electrocardiograph and claimed to have discovered a yogi who could stop his heart. But not everyone took her seriously; and only in the last couple of decades have more widely recognized studies been performed. Among these one of the most striking was that of Dr and Mrs Elmer Green in 1970, with Swami Rama, a yogi from Rishikesh in the Himalayas. A man in his middle forties, Swami Rama had been practising Yoga since the age of four.

In a report issued from the Menninger Foundation, Dr Green describes in considerable detail the swami's remarkable ability to regulate bodily functions ordinarily outside human control (Green (6)). For example, in a preliminary interview the swami showed such control of blood-flow that he caused two areas on the palm of his right hand to change temperature in opposite directions – one part became ashen grey and the other bright red. Later in the laboratory he stopped his heart from pumping blood for at least seventeen seconds in what Dr Green describes as an 'atrial flutter' which ordinarily causes death. He also produced at will alpha and theta waves, subsequently telling the researchers about his interior state during these exercises. He was able to diagnose physical ailments in others. And finally he lay down with his eyes closed and, while gently snoring, produced the delta rhythm characteristic of deep sleep. Yet after twenty-five minutes he opened his eyes and repeated almost verbatim everything that had been said while he was 'asleep'. He called this a 'yogic sleep' during which he had told his mind to record everything that was happening while his brain slept. All the above has been documented with scientific rigour by Dr and Mrs Elmer Green.

Swami Rama is obviously an exceptional man. At Harvard, however, experiments of a more modest kind were performed upon practitioners of transcendental meditation with no pretensions to extraordinary powers. The subjects tested were mainly young people between the ages of twenty and thirty who had been practising TM from anything between six months and three years (Segal, p. 377).

Results showed that from the physiological and metabolic standpoint meditation is deeply restful, more so than the ordinary relaxation found through lounging in a chair. In this latter situation there remains considerable muscle tension which is relaxed in time of meditation. Meditation, the researchers claimed, is a form of relaxation quite as natural to man as sleep or rest. Concretely they showed that after a few minutes of meditation the breathing slowed down, oxygen consumption was reduced, carbon-dioxide elimination declined. Blood-pressure also dropped and the heart beat more slowly. Skin resistance to electricity was measured by means of electrodes taped to the hands. It is well known that in a state of anxiety skin resistance to electricity drops (and on this principle the lie detector works) but in meditation skin resistance was shown to increase fivefold. Moreover lactate concentration in the blood declined, again showing a lowering of anxiety. Brainwaves registered high-amplitude alpha as in Zen; and all in all the claim of the researchers that meditation is deeply restful seemed to have ample foundation. One more extremely significant point was the number of meditators who claimed to have abandoned drug-abuse after starting meditation.

Studies performed on Zen in Tokyo showed very similar results. It was found that Zen is a deeply restful state in which blood-pressure falls, the heart beats more slowly than usual, anxiety is reduced and high-amplitude alpha is recorded on the EEG.

All this points to a fascinating conclusion; namely, that the person who meditates becomes physiologically different from the person who does not. Brain rhythms, heart-beat, blood-pressure, skin resistance – all are changed by meditation. And researchers have told me that people who go off to make a week's *sesshin* often return physiologically different. The great religious traditions, of course, have seen this intuitively and that is why people who meditate have instinctively taken on a different diet, different clothes, different sleeping habits and a different life-style. They have discovered that certain occupations are incompatible with the meditational thrust that fills their life; and sometimes they have made a strange option for celibacy. This confirms a point I have constantly made throughout this book; namely, that meditation is not just an occupation taken on night and morning for several hours each day. It is a whole way of life or, more correctly, a way of being. Once one gets into it, it tends to take over, to change and to transform. Anybody starting it had better sit down and count the cost like the sensible man who wants to build a tower.

In regard to the physiological benefits gained from meditation it is interesting to try to pinpoint the precise health-giving dimension. Some researchers in Tokyo have claimed that the beneficial effects stem from the lotus posture. They refer to the straight back, the balanced position, the slightly touching fingers and the slow breathing as conducive to the deepest human relaxation. Furthermore they claim that next to the lying-down position, the lotus is the posture in which the least energy is expended. All this contains much truth; and I believe that scientific studies on the flow of blood to the brain and the relaxation of muscle tension will reveal more and more the physiological benefits of the lotus. At the same time, I think it would be an exaggeration to put all the emphasis here and here only because similar benefits are reaped in transcendental meditation and other systems that do not insist on the lotus. Moreover, even in Zen the lotus posture, though highly desirable, is not essential. Zen can be practised on a sick-bed. Consequently we must look elsewhere for an explanation of the therapeutic dimension of meditation.

I myself believe that the secret lies in what scientists now call *passive concentration* and *passive energy*. This is a newly discovered energy which promises to be of immense significance for the future of science and for the future of man. It was introduced to the scientific world by the German scientist Joannes Schultz whose autogenic training (influenced by Western medicine, by hypnosis and by Yoga) first gained popularity in Europe around the year 1910. But before examining passive energy in detail I would like to glance at its role in meditational therapy.

The significance of experiments like that with Swami Rama does not precisely lie in the possibility of stopping one's heart or performing extraordinary feats. What is significant is the possibility of creating a new form of therapy through body-control. If people can learn to regulate body-temperature, blood-flow, heart-rate, and so on, enormous possibilities are opened in psychosomatic medicine. And if it is demonstrated that the automatic or involuntary nervous system is not involuntary after all, new vistas may well be opened.

At the Menninger Foundation in Kansas, volunteers are now being taught to control internal states by means of biofeedback, using audio and visual displays (Segal, p. 302). The method is rather similar to that which I described when speaking of control of brain rhythms. In regard to the regulation of hyper-tension, for example, the subject is wired to the machine in such a way that a light flashes any time his blood-pressure rises above a certain point. His job, then, is to prevent that light from flashing and so keep down his blood-pressure. It has been discovered that will-power or *active volition* (willing, willing that my blood-pressure go down) achieves nothing or may even have the contrary effect. But if I wish that my blood-pressure go down in a passive way and then simply allow the thing to happen – in this way, and by the use of biofeedback, I may attain to a great deal of control. The secret lies in the control of passive energy and the exercise of *passive volition*. And the whole process is a species of meditation.

A wide variety of experiments with this kind of therapy are being performed. There is, for example, training in muscle relaxation. It is known that in the process of relaxation the muscles in the forehead are of primary significance – if they are relaxed, a total relaxation becomes possible. So an electrode is pasted to the forehead, and when the muscle relaxes a light flashes or the meter goes down. And in this way muscle relaxation is learned. But the result is achieved not by striving and straining actively, but by passive volition.

Or again there is the possibility of curing migraine headaches. It was discovered that relief could be achieved through increasing the flow of blood to the hands in what is called 'hand warming'. Once again, active volition, with strong and determined resolutions that 'I *will* warm my hands', achieves nothing; but if one relaxes, wishes the thing to happen and then allows it to happen, extraordinary results can be achieved. As before, electrodes are pasted to the hands and hooked up to a meter which immediately registers the slightest change in temperature. In this way the patient is immediately informed when his hands begin to get warm and can learn to regulate the temperature for himself: he is learning the art of passive volition.

It is still too early to predict the future of this new branch of medicine based on passive concentration and meditation. The suggestion has been made that a cure for cancer could conceivably be found – that voluntary starvation and absorption of cancerous growths through blood-flow control is within the realm of possibility. However that may be, one of the most significant aspects of it all is that we are coming to a form of medicine in which the patient will heal himself and in which the role of doctors and nurses will be radically changed. It seems to me that there is something right about this. It makes healing creative and positive rather than a process to be undergone.

From what has been said it will be clear that passive energy is not necessarily religious. It can be generated in a meditational therapy that has nothing to do with religious faith. Or it can be found to predominate in certain cultures. In Japan, for example, it is un-mistakably present in the tea-ceremony, the flower arrangement, calligraphy, and even in traditional sports like judo and archery.

But it is found pre-eminently in religious meditation from ancient times. The *Bhagavad Gita* tells us to work without coveting the fruits of our labour. In other words, we want the fruit but we don't strain and strive to obtain it. In a sense we don't want it at all, and we are wholly detached. This is an example of passive volition. Or again, in Zen one's aim is *satori*. Yet one does not strive and strain for this experience; and if one does so, one will not get it. The striving must be done in a passive way – and this again is passive volition. In Christian contemplation, too, the love of God brings about a cessation of thought and a consequent generation of passive energy. Clearly in all these cases the passive energy is associated with (and is perhaps the cause of) the high-amplitude alpha that registers on the EEG of contemplative meditators. It is important to note, however, that religious meditation differs from meditational therapy in that it has a totally different motivation and (in most religions) a belief in the action of a divine power and in his grace. This changes the exercise radically: passive energy is no more than a psychological consequence of a deeper spiritual aspiration and communion that can never be measured.

But in either case the psychological process is similar. One goes beyond discursive reasoning and yet remains alert and aware. Here is the core of passive energy. It is found in a state of consciousness where the mind does not go out to an object in order to analyse it in a discursive way. Rather does it take in the whole to 'contemplate' (literally 'gaze upon') and identify with it. Passive energy belongs to the intuitive way of thinking just as active energy belongs to the discursive. Both are necessary for full human development.

This passive energy, then, may go in many directions. It is principally in Yoga that it is directed to body-control. The lotus posture (and this I believe is very significant) is a magnificent way to the fostering of passive energy. By sitting in the lotus position and entering deeply into Yoga one can become aware of one's body in a new way. One can become conscious of physiological functions that normally pass unobserved. Not only is one conscious of the breathing, but one may also listen to the heart-beat and, it is claimed, one may come to an awareness of digestion, metabolism and one's whole interior physiology. Having become aware of them by *passive concentration*, the next step is to control them by *passive volition*. But in the highest spiritual traditions of Yoga, such control of bodily functions is considered of little importance compared with the great ideal of union with the divine.

In truly religious exercises passive energy is something like a vehicle for the activity of the Spirit – an activity that transcends all measurable energy. Sometimes it is found in group prayer – the vibrations that unite the participants are almost palpable. Or it can exist between two persons. In the East the interesting word *darshan* speaks of the communion that can exist in a deeply spiritual contact between two people, usually master and disciple. Or the same exchange of energy can be found between two people who are in love: their communion is intuitive, beyond all words and discourse in a kind of fusion of consciousnesses. I would hazard the guess that passive energy plays a key role in clairvoyance, mind-reading, telepathy and other forms of extrasensory perception. But, I repeat, it is not necessarily religious. Probably it is generated in large quantities in mass hysteria, and it could be used for evil as well as for good. What makes it religious is the further 'super-energy' of grace and profound motivation.

The scientific discovery of passive energy may well turn out to be a major breakthrough in our day. For one thing it demonstrates to the scientist that the Carmelite monastery, the Carthusian hermitage, the Hindu ashram and the Zen temple are not a refuge for people who want to waste time. They are generating large quantities of a very high and precious energy. What happens to that energy and how it is used is another matter. I myself believe that it is the material basis for a higher, unmeasurable, spiritual energy that builds the earth.

10. *The healing of the mind*

In the last chapter I distinguished between meditational therapy on the one hand and religious meditation on the other. It was not my intention to make a value judgement, as though one were better than the other. Rather did I mean that they are different in much the same way as psychology and theology are different, if overlapping, sciences. To aim at producing a state of consciousness that will heal body or mind is a legitimate and laudable aim of meditational therapy. But religious meditation does not do this. It strives for ultimates. That it may also have therapeutic consequences (St John of the Cross speaks of the cure of bad humours) and that it may also embrace psychological goals is a point I wish to make later; but even in this case the healing cannot be ascribed solely to the psychological process. Other factors enter in.

Before speaking of its healing power, let me recall that meditation is not necessarily therapeutic. In *The Psychophysiology of Zen* Dr Tomio Hirai observes that many neurotics visit Zen temples in Japan in search of psychological health. But quite often they get sicker. He then states that Zen should not be recommended for the emotionally unbalanced or for those with latent psychoses. Such people may find it impossible to integrate the images and problems released from the unconscious. Besides, Dr Hirai feels that the great severity of Zen in its present form renders it unsuitable for the masses.

Yet some kinds of meditation, including a modified form of Zen, do seem to be beneficial and therapeutic for certain people. For example, as mentioned in the last chapter, transcendental meditation sometimes helps cure drug-abuse. Or again, in *The Still Point* I spoke about a Japanese psychiatrist who combines *zazen* with counselling (Johnston (2), pp. 59–60). Or again, it has been claimed that simply by entering into prolonged alpha consciousness through biofeedback a cure for neurosis has been effected. Wherein lies the therapeutic dimension of the meditational practice? This is the question I would first like to ask. And perhaps a clue is provided by considering the role of the memory in man's psychic life.

It is now axiomatic in psychology that most neuroses and emotional disturbances are connected with the memory. While we are still desperately ignorant about the millions of cells within the brain, one clear thing is that our past is recorded and stored and can be played back in the present. In other words, the brain is like a tape-recorder that retains every experience we have had since birth – and, perhaps, since before birth.

All this is colourfully expressed in transactional analysis, which tells us that within us, stored in our memory, are a Parent and a Child.[1] The latter is an obstreperous, neurotic child who causes trouble and anguish and fear, telling us we are not OK and building our inferiority complex. And side by side with him is a finger-wagging, legalistic parent who torments us with warnings, admonitions and unreasonable prejudices. If we want to make balanced decisions, the Adult within must be in control and we must not be dominated by the Parent and the Child. We cannot entirely get rid of these voices from the past. They are engrained in the tape-recorder of memory. But we can learn to be detached from them, to be uninfluenced by them. We can smile compassionately at our neurotic Child and say, 'There he goes again!' Or we can ignore and by-pass the crushing admonitions of the Parent.

Whatever way we want to express it, the fact is that ghosts inhabit our memory, influencing our present conduct. And in order to be healed we must find some way of confronting them, or handling them, or being detached from them.

Now certain forms of meditation make a great impact on the memory and can effect a detachment from interior states of consciousness. Probably any meditation which brings us into high-amplitude alpha stimulates and brings to the surface half-buried memories. This, at all events, seems to follow from the results of certain memory tests made by Dr Green in which the alpha-producers had better scores (Segal, p. 304; Green (1)). One can understand how this could be so. In the kind of meditation that goes beyond discursive thinking into a new level of awareness, thoughts and feelings from the past may rise to the surface of the mind. The not-OK Child may shriek and shout. The Parent may complain and admonish. Half-buried fears may float up from the unconscious. But I pay no attention to these troublesome voices from the past because

---

[1] *I'm OK – You're OK* by Thomas Harris.

I have entered a deeper level of mind where I can be detached and silent and free from their domination.

And now a cure may be effected in any of several ways.

One is by the help of an analyst or counsellor with whom I confront the ghosts and goblins, driving them away or weakening their power over me. In this case, it will immediately be seen, the meditational process is a rather secondary thing. It is little more than a preparation or a way to discover the hidden problems. It has played a role somewhat similar to that of the couch. The psychoanalyst is the central actor in the drama.

But there is another possibility. It may be that I find such joy and satisfaction at my new level of awareness that the howling Child and the grumbling Parent no longer bother me. They shout themselves to death, or die of exposure, or they starve. And I am liberated and healed. Perhaps the awareness of my problems (while at the same time letting them be) leads to a kind of enlightenment in their regard and they lose their power. As Rollo May says, the demon is named; and having been named, he loses his power.

Yet another possibility is that the joy emanating from my new level of awareness is so great that lesser fixations become unimportant. Entrance into deeper states of consciousness through meditation produces psychophysiological effects of joy and calmness and integration which are the positive side of what is happening negatively in the memory. This calmness is a great treasure. It is found in transcendental meditation and may explain why TM sometimes cures drug-abuse: the new joy makes the drug experience look trivial.

At the same time I myself believe that the technique of entering into deeper levels of consciousness alone will not heal the mind in a human way. This healing will never be complete without the presence of two factors that are extraneous to the meditational process.

The first of these is love. It is a truism to say that people need to be loved and are not infrequently sick from lack of love. This is particularly true of the child, which may well die if not loved. Love is the great healer; and meditational therapy will not be complete without love from counsellor or friend or family or community.

The second is meaning. Jung, Viktor Frankl and the rest stress that no cure will be complete unless a man finds motivation and a reason for living. Meditation itself does not provide motivation. This must come from elsewhere.

In other words, even on the psychological plane, a mere technique of meditation (whether it be the recitation of a *mantra*, or the counting of the breathing, or the adoption of a given posture) will never effect a total cure. It may give temporary relief; but the deepest self of man calls for more.

Mention of love and meaning brings me to religion. As I have already said, religious meditation does not aim at therapy. But it can have therapeutic consequences; and its psychological pattern is similar to that of the meditational therapy already outlined. Let me illustrate this from Christian contemplation.

Christian contemplation is the answer to a call and the response to a vision. One cannot embark on the journey until one has heard the voice or glimpsed the footprints of the ox. In other words there is an initial awakening. One stops in one's tracks, amazed by the realization that one is loved. Christian contemplation begins with the belief, the conviction, the experience of God's love for me. It never starts with vigorous efforts on my part; it does not manifest itself through active energy; it does not begin with my violently drumming up some powerful love for God and man. This is stated explicitly by John: 'In this is love, not that we loved God but that he loved us' (1 John 4:10). This love powerfully experienced has been compared to the call of the good shepherd inviting us to enter the sheepfold.

Now this call is creative. It creates a response, an interior movement, a motion of love that necessarily expresses itself in an altered state of consciousness. So deep is the call and so interior is my response that a new level of awareness is opened up and I enter into a changed environment. Christian contemplation is the experience of being loved and of loving at the most profound level of psychic life and of spirit.

This love is not directed to some imaginary world of escape beyond the senses. Rather does it go out to the great reality of the cosmic, risen Christ who loves me and whom I love. This is the Christ who is before our very eyes and ears and hearts and whose glory is all around us because he is 'the mountains, the solitary wooded valleys, strange islands . . . silent music', and the people I meet every day.

The love affair thus initiated lasts until death and beyond death.

It goes on and on. Sometimes it is violent and anguishing like the struggle of Jacob and the angel: at other times it is a peaceful reclining in the arms of the beloved: 'His left arm . . . under my head' and 'his right arm embrac[ing] me' (Song of Solomon 2:6). One enters new mansions: new areas of psychic life are opened up.

Examining the development of this love affair, one immediately sees its psychological similarity to the meditational therapy already described.

First of all there is the entrance into a deeper level of awareness under the gentle guidance of the Spirit. When this happens, the mind is expanded, the unconscious is opened up and (just as in meditational therapy) ghosts and goblins, as well as saints and angels, may rise up from the unconscious. The memory is stimulated. The past becomes luminous. The obstreperous Child and the admonishing Parent begin to raise their voices with excitement and clamour. Joy and sadness, love and hate may surge up. The meditator is aware of all this. But he lets it be. He pays no attention to it. He refuses to engage in any analysis of this turmoil. He will not have dialogue with it because the deepest centre of his being, beating on the cloud of unknowing with the shaft of love, is imbibing exquisite wisdom of a supraconceptual kind. It is this love that is all-important to him. As for the ghosts from the unconscious, they may shout themselves to death or they may die of exposure and neglect. Or the wounds from the past, now exposed to the healing power of the Spirit, may be beautifully transfigured – 'because God's love has been poured into our hearts through the Holy Spirit which has been given to us' (Romans 5:5).

The angry rising of the ghosts and goblins is well expressed in *The Book of Privy Counselling*:

Do not be overcome with anxious dread if the evil one comes (as he will) with sudden fierceness, knocking and hammering on the walls of your house; or if he should stir some of his mighty agents to rise suddenly and attack you without warning. Let us be clear about this: the fiend must be taken into account. Anyone beginning this work (I do not care who he is) is liable to feel, smell, taste or hear some surprising effects concocted by the enemy in one or other of his senses. So do not be astonished if it happens. There is nothing he will not try to drag you down from the heights of such valuable work.   (Johnston (1), ch. 7)

Without denying the existence of the fiend, all the author says can equally be applied to the tantrums of the neurotic Child and the admonitions of the dominating Parent, whose voices from the past may be working to destroy our house and wreck our true love. It is precisely by allowing them to ramp and rage, by compassionately acknowledging them but paying no attention to them, that their power is diminished and a cure is effected.

And how stable and rooted is the meditator! The schizophrenic and the drug addict, it is true, may enter similar levels of awareness; but in the ensuing turmoil their Adult is frequently tossed out of the saddle while the neurotic Child takes over. But the mystic is less easily dislodged. He is guided by love. 'Nought but my love to be my guide', writes St John of the Cross.

So his great stability continues to stem from the knowledge that he is loved. It is to this faith that the Adult silently clings when the not-OK Child and the Parent are screaming their heads off; and it is this that makes the meditation therapeutic. Moreover (and this is important) the faith that forms the very core of Christian meditation is not faith that I am loved *because* I am good and holy and sinless; it is belief that I am deeply loved *in spite of* my sinfulness. So says Paul: 'God shows his love for us in that while we were yet sinners Christ died for us' (Romans 5:8). Yahweh does not love his people because they are holy (how often they are unfaithful and stiff-necked!) but in order to make them holy. And this is the faith the meditator clings to in his journey into the profound caverns of the unconscious. If he loses this, he loses everything. His faith is not primarily a belief that God exists but that God loves; and it is this love that sustains him: 'Because you are precious in my eyes . . . and I love you . . .' (Isaiah 43:4).

Now my point in this chapter is that this religious conviction of being loved is therapeutic in its consequences, a point made also by Thomas Harris in his best-selling work on transactional analysis. In an excellent chapter (which, the introduction tells us, was written by his wife) he comes to the crucial point of his work: how am I to come to the conviction that *I'm OK*? And he answers that this security comes from the realization that I am loved – and this, he says, is ultimately a religious experience. It is an experience of grace which, for Paul Tillich, means that I am unconditionally loved. Concretely, I come to the realization that *I'm OK* through a conversion experience like that of Paul: 'The Son of God . . . loved me and gave himself for me!' (Galatians 2:20)

But it is not only the experience of being loved that is therapeutic. The very response to love is therapeutic too. This answering love, as has been pointed out, is not directed towards some abstraction but towards the living, risen, cosmic Christ who is in our friends and our enemies, who is in the poor and the sick and the afflicted. And the experience of loving him in himself and in others, no less than the experience of being loved, is therapeutic in its consequences because it purifies the whole person – mind and memory and unconscious. When one begins to love profoundly at a new level of awareness (as often happens in deep intimacy between a man and a woman) it may happen that latent or repressed forces rise to the surface of the mind: hatred, jealousy, fear, insecurity, anger, suspicion, anxiety, unbridled eroticism and the rest surge up from the murky depths of the unconscious. And all this, it is well known, can coexist with true love. This violence, unleashed in human relations, can be unleashed also in the divine – the two are not so distinct, and divine love is incarnate. And one is liberated only by continuing to love. By fixing one's heart on the cloud of unknowing with deep peace, one becomes detached from these turbulent uprisings; and then they wither and die, leaving only love. It is by loving at the ultimate point, by going beyond all categories to the deepest centre, that one is liberated from jealousy and hatred and the rest. But this is an agonizing purification.

All this is particularly evident in that form of love which we call forgiveness. Most psychologists will agree that one of the most damaging traumas that can exist in the memory is suppressed anger and refusal to forgive. Because of early wounds, people refuse to accept others (you're not OK) and to accept themselves (I'm not OK) and end up in emotional upheaval. Often the root problem is an unconscious refusal to love and forgive their parents. And this makes it difficult to love and forgive anyone: because we are for ever projecting parental images on to the people we meet. One may succeed in forgiving in the conscious mind (and this is enough for salvation) but the unconscious lags behind, leaving our love so much less human.

But through meditation a deeper level of awareness is opened up. Love and faith, if only they are present, can now seep down into the more profound caverns of consciousness and into the subtler layers of the mind, enabling one to love and to forgive with a totality that was hitherto unthinkable. At the deep centre now reached, one can pass beyond parental projections, childhood fears, and other obstructions, to meet the person of the other. When this is done and one forgives from the core of one's being, an enlightenment takes place in a moment of total reconciliation with the universe. Barriers fall down; no one and no thing is rejected; all is one. In the act of forgiveness one realizes that one is forgiven; one loses self-hatred (which is the source of every other hatred); one is healed in an act of love.

From all this it is clear that the principal element in healing is not the psychological process and the entrance into internal states of consciousness. If that were so, drugs alone might heal. But what is really therapeutic is the faith and love which penetrate these deeper internal states. What is therapeutic is the experience of loving and being loved.

Finally, it is important to recall what is meant by healing. It is not the restoration of some stereotyped normality or social adaptability. It is not that the past is obliterated. It is not that wounds are patched up and the torn flesh restored to its pristine health. Neither will healing necessarily make the homosexual heterosexual; it will not give the alcoholic a taste for Coca-Cola. Healing is much more creative than that.

No, healing is progress and resurrection. It can best be understood by looking at the wounds of the risen Christ. These are still present. The resurrection did not take them away. But they are glorified, transformed, transfigured. Now they are beautiful: 'Put your finger here, and see my hands; and put out your hand, and place it in my side . . .' (John 20:27). And in the same way meditation can remove the crippling effects of painful wounds and it can make beautiful what once was ugly. And it can give to the personality such depth of love and profundity of insight that the ghosts no longer frighten and the sirens no longer seduce.

And then comes the liberation of the true self. When the Parent and the neurotic Child have perished from exhaustion or neglect, the natural Child, nurtured by this great love, rises up from the depth of one's being. This Child, unlike the other neurotic, is innocent, wondering, religious, artistic – the source of creativity. This is the contemplative Child who is the subject of *samadhi* and ecstasy and the prayer of quiet. He now begins to love and to sing and to dance and to beget beauty. But above all, he cries out, 'Abba! Father!' And in that moment of awakening we are healed.

Yet just as enlightenment is never complete in this world, neither is healing complete. More about this in the next chapter.

11. *The deeper healing*

From what has been said it will be clear that the healing power of meditation drives its roots deep down into the unconscious caverns of the mind, effecting a cure that can be physical or psychological. At the same time, it is an obvious fact that not everyone who meditates is a model of physical and psychological health. We know that many monks, both Christian and Buddhist, suffer from ulcers, malnutrition, consumption, and even from neurosis. The crippling effects of this neurosis, I have tried to say, may be removed. The whole thing may be transfigured – but the neurosis itself may somehow remain for life. St Paul was constantly sick, in addition to having some affliction which scripture scholars do not understand. 'And to keep me from being too elated by the abundance of revelations, a thorn was given me in the flesh, a messenger of Satan, to harass me, to keep me from being too elated. Three times I besought the Lord about this, that it should leave me; but he said to me, "My grace is sufficient for you, for my power is made perfect in weakness." I will all the more gladly boast of my weaknesses, that the power of Christ may rest upon me' (2 Corinthians 12:7-9). This is a good example of a true healing which might not satisfy the local doctor. Healing there is, because Paul is cured of his pride and his tendency to be elated, while within him a new power, the power of Christ, arises. Yet, on the other hand, this healing does not come the way Paul wants.

The fact is that while all the great religions claim to heal, this healing process is often paradoxical, to such an extent that death cures and sickness strengthens.

But before going into that, let us ask ourselves about the basic sickness of man. What precisely is wrong with the human race?

If we were to ask psychology about modern man's basic sickness, we might hear that it is the sense of meaninglessness, of emptiness, of ultimate frustration. How agonizingly this was expressed by philosophers between the two wars with their talk of existential anguish and all the suffering summed up by Heidegger's terrible definition of man as 'being-to-death'! Confronted with death, man

is aware of his contingency, his incompleteness, his imperfection –
and it is this that fills him with existential dread. So he has to find
meaning. Not just meaning for his economic, or emotional or cultural
life, but meaning for his existence. Hence Viktor Frankl's logotherapy. Hence Teilhard's affirmation of 'Omega', the point of
convergence and the term of evolution. Without this, claims Teilhard,
there is no meaning to the whole business of life.

Or some philosophers might tell us that man's basic problem is his
tendency to hate his fellow-men, his tendency to recoil from them in
the Sartrian conviction that hell is the other. There is something
destructive in man, a strange mixture of love and hate.

Now the great religions have never failed to recognize man's basic
sickness and have attempted to give meaning to this puzzling
predicament called human existence. They uniformly claim that
man's existential problems run deeper than his chemistry and his
psyche, existing as they do at the very root of his being. Let me say a
word about both Buddhism and Christianity in this regard.

The Buddhist attitude to man's basic sickness is formulated in *The
Four Noble Truths*, which may be summarized as follows:

(1) Existence is unhappiness
(2) Unhappiness is caused by self-centred desire
(3) Self-centred desire can be destroyed
(4) It can be destroyed by following the eightfold path
    which is that of
        Right views
        Right intentions
        Right speech
        Right conduct
        Right livelihood
        Right effort
        Right mindfulness
        Right concentration

'Existence is unhappiness'! This sounds like the existential anguish
of the philosophers; and it is an emphasis that echoes all through
Buddhism. Man is in illusion; man is suffering. Here are a few words
from the famous *Fire Sermon*, reputedly preached by the Buddha at
Benares after his great enlightenment:

All things, O priests, are on fire. And what, O priests, are all these things that are on fire?

The eye, O priests, is on fire; forms are on fire; eye-consciousness is on fire; impressions received by the eye are on fire; and whatever sensation, pleasant, unpleasant, or indifferent, originates in dependence on impressions received by the eye, that also is on fire. And with what are these on fire? With the fire of passion, say I, with the fire of hatred, with the fire of infatuation; with birth, old age, death, sorrow, lamentation, misery, grief, and despair are they on fire.   (Burtt, p. 97)

And so it goes on, depicting eye and ear and nose and tongue and body and mind and ideas and impressions, all on fire.

I said that this resembles the anguish of the philosophers. But there is one important difference: Buddhism holds out hope of salvation. It indicates that there is a way out of the mess. Man can be saved from his existential suffering by the eightfold path of right views, right intentions, right speech, and all the rest. Here Buddhism asks for faith – faith that the situation is not hopeless, faith that there is a way out, faith that there is some meaning to it all, faith that man can be healed. And then faith that this eightfold path really does lead to the highest wisdom, *prajna*, through which man is liberated, saved, brought to *nirvana*. It is to this *prajna* or awakening or enlightenment that all forms of Buddhism point; and it is to the everlasting credit of the Buddha to have reminded the world that man is liberated through wisdom – beyond images and concepts, in the total cessation of desire. 'The truth will make you free' (John 8:32).

It is worth noting here that in Buddhism the way to healing wisdom is not precisely meditation but the eightfold path. This is because, in the best Buddhist (as in the best Judaeo-Christian) tradition, meditation is not just a period of silent wall-gazing. Rather is it life. Zen is not just 'sitting' or *zazen;* it is also eating, sleeping, walking, working and life. At the same time, 'right concentration' does hold a privileged place in this life; and for this reason Buddhism is rightly symbolized by the majestic statues of the Buddha, deep in meditation and rising into the serenity of wisdom, as the lotus rises to the sunlight out of the dark, muddy pond.

A striking parallel to this Buddhist philosophy is found in Romans. In Tokyo I once had occasion to read this epistle with some Japanese students. I was amazed at their interest and their insights. Only later did it dawn on me that this might be because of its striking similarity to the Buddhist philosophy that is the backbone of their culture. With what vigour does Paul paint man in the mire! 'They were filled with all manner of wickedness, evil, covetousness, malice. Full of envy, murder, strife, deceit, malignity, they are gossips, slanderers, haters of God, insolent, haughty, boastful, inventors of evil, disobedient to parents, foolish, faithless, heartless, ruthless' (Romans 1:29–31). With a masterly command of words and a rich vocabulary Paul depicts in lurid terms the Roman Empire of his day. And it was not only the Empire that needed salvation. Jew, Greek, Gentile, everyone was in the mess. For Paul is here describing the situation that subsequently came to be called *original sin*.

And again he asks the Buddhist question: Is there a way out? Is there salvation? How is man to escape from this anguished situation? How can he be healed? And once again he gives an answer which recalls that of the Buddha. Man is liberated or 'justified' by faith. Romans plays on the theme that 'he who through faith is righteous shall live' (Romans 1:17).

When he comes to explaining in more detail what this faith is, of course, Paul parts company with Buddhism. For him it is faith in God's love, based upon a historical fact: 'While we were still weak, at the right time Christ died for the ungodly. Why, one will hardly die for a righteous man – though perhaps for a good man one will dare even to die. But God shows his love for us in that while we were yet sinners Christ died for us' (Romans 5:6–8). Faith in God's love and the saving death of his Son is the way to salvation.

But the parallel with Buddhism continues in that Paul does not situate this faith in long periods of wall-gazing meditation. For him, also, faith is life. Rather than define it philosophically he simply tells the story of Abraham, pointing to the great patriarch's life as an example of living faith (Romans 4:1–4). Yes, faith is life, like the life of Abraham. And meditation (which is no more than an exercise of faith) is also life. As in Buddhism it is a life that leads to wisdom; but for Paul the wisdom that liberates and heals is Jesus Christ himself, who is 'the power of God and the wisdom of God' (1 Corinthians 1:24). This is the risen Jesus who can only be grasped by love in an act that is beyond concepts and images in a new dimension transcending thought.

Both Buddhism and Christianity, then, situate man's sickness at a deeper level than migraine headaches, high blood-pressure and getting stuck in the Oedipus conflict. It is man's very existence that is somehow vitiated, and his existential anguish flows from a metaphysical sickness at the level of being. When we come to ask more in detail about man's ugly plight, we find *The Four Noble Truths* attributing the evil to self-centred desire. In Buddhism the great enemy is the self, which cuts man off from the all, separates him from the totality, hurls him into the illusion of multiplicity. And so this self must be annihilated if one is to enter *nirvana*.

In Christianity the root problem is original sin. What precisely this means, however, is far from clear today. Recent advances in anthropology and in biblical studies have made theologians rethink the old doctrine of 'the fall'. It is hardly possible here to enter into their theories and niceties. Enough to say that when the smoke clears, the new thinking does not negate but reaffirms the basic traditional truth; namely, that man is in a sorry plight and needs salvation.

I myself believe that we find the most graphic account of original sin and its healing in the very heart of Paul. The Epistle to the Romans tells us of an existential struggle that runs deeper than the sharp physical pain that came as Satan's messenger. For this struggle is at the root of Paul's being – at the level of the self. Paul never sets himself above us; he never poses as the enlightened man; he never says that he has arrived. He is in the hurly-burly with the rest of us. And so in vivid words he describes the anguished struggle between the two selves at the depth of his being. 'I do not understand my own actions. For I do not do what I want, but I do the very thing I hate . . . I do not do the good I want, but the evil I do not want is what I do' (Romans 7:15, 19). And he cries out for existential healing: 'Wretched man that I am! Who will deliver me from this body of death?' (Romans 7:24)

Who will deliver Paul? The answer is Christ. He is the great healer, just as in his historical existence he cured the blind and the sick and the lame and the deaf to symbolize a deeper healing at the existential level of the self. Paul fixes his eyes on Jesus whom he loves and runs after him like the athletes in the Hellenistic games, they for the corruptible crown, Paul for the incorruptible. 'I press on toward the goal for the prize of the upward call of God in Christ Jesus' (Philippians 3:14). Every Pauline line vibrates with Christ's love for Paul and Paul's love for Christ. For him life is a love affair with the risen, universal, cosmic Christ. 'I betrothed you to Christ to present you as a pure bride to her one husband', he writes to the Corinthians (2 Corinthians 11:2), and just as the faithful are the bride of the risen Christ, so is Paul. And in this is he not the fore-runner of one whose beloved is 'the mountains, the solitary wooded valleys, strange islands . . . silent music'? It is this love which drives Paul; it is this love which heals him. 'Who shall separate us from the love of Christ?' (Romans 8:35) As if to say that Christ's love is an irresistible force or a blinding light from which there is no escape. And Paul must share in this love and make it his own: 'If I speak in the tongues of men and of angels, but have not love, I am a noisy gong or a clanging cymbal' (1 Corinthians 13:1).

The Christ who heals is the risen Jesus, now alive and intimately present to Paul and to all who believe. It is towards the risen Christ that he runs; and before his eyes stands out the second coming, the *parousia*. Now Christ is Lord, *Kyrios;* his is a name that is above all names; he is the cosmic centre towards which the human race is moving. Just as Christ rose, so will Paul rise. Just as Christ was transfigured, Paul will be transfigured. And this is the ultimate healing. Man is cured from his existential anguish and separation by union with the risen Christ and by resurrection with him. In the last analysis it is only the resurrection that heals.

But prior to resurrection is inevitable anguish and pain – prin-cipally the pain of separation. Paul longs and longs for the termination of this separation. He wants to leap over the gap that separates him from his beloved. 'My desire is to depart and be with Christ, for that is far better . . . For to me to live is Christ, and to die is gain' (Philippians 1:23, 21). And so he longs for death. Not that he is in love with death itself (that would be morbid) but he sees it as the gateway to resurrection. 'Far be it from me to glory except in the cross of our Lord Jesus Christ, by which the world has been crucified to me, and I to the world' (Galatians 6:14). Christ's death and resurrection are one single, inseparable, dramatic event. It might be nice to separate them; it might be nice to choose Christ's resurrection and forget about his death. But Paul knows that this cannot be. He must go through the whole process with Christ: '. . . that I . . . may share his sufferings, becoming like him in his death, that if possible I may attain the resurrection from the dead' (Philippians 3:10–11).

Death, being the one gateway to the resurrection, is glorious. What most people see as the great enemy is now transfigured in the golden light of the resurrection. Now it is a conquered enemy:

> Death is swallowed up in victory.
> O death, where is thy victory?
> O death, where is thy sting? (1 Corinthians 15:54–55)

Not only death but all that precedes it is transfigured. Hence Paul can glory in the cross and in his crucifixion to the world. Moreover, if we are moving towards him whom we love, then the other things in life are much less important. And the consequence is an almost absurd detachment. 'Let those who have wives live as though they had none, and those who mourn as though they were not mourning, and those who rejoice as though they were not rejoicing, and those who buy as though they had no goods, and those who deal with the world as though they had no dealings with it' (1 Corinthians 7:29–31). What ridiculous detachment! It can only be explained in the light of an overwhelming desire for, and expectation of, the coming of one whom Paul loves more than life itself.

So Paul sings a paean of salvation, of love, of healing – which ends with the resurrection and the coming of him who is the soul of Paul's soul. He never loses sight of the goal; he never forgets the resurrection If he were to do so, the whole fabric would collapse. 'If for this life only we have hoped in Christ, we are of all men most to be pitied' (1 Corinthians 15:19). His is a song of triumph; but he never glories in the cross unless in the background there shines the resurrection.

Paul is the prototype of the Christian mystic. Those who follow sing the same song of love. They, too, love Christ unto foolishness; they, too, desire death and they glory in the cross that they may attain to the resurrection. They, too, fascinated by the divine eyes, throw off everything and run naked towards the goal where they are clothed in Christ. They, too, see their healing in the resurrection. This, I say, is the doctrine of the great Christian mystics. But the lesser people, the writers of little books and the composers of pious treatises often saw Paul glorying in the cross and they forgot about his greater glory – in the resurrection. And so a somewhat morbid doctrine of suffering and 'love of the cross' crept into the Christian message. Morbid, because to glory in the cross while forgetting the resurrection is the stupidity of stupidities. 'If for this life only we

have hoped in Christ, we are of all men most to be pitied' (1 Corinthians 15:19).

Extremes bring reaction. Because of a morbid understanding of
suffering and detachment and the like, some modern Christians tend
to reject the whole thing. Detachment has become an ugly word and
suffering is no longer a thing in which to glory. This is unfortunate.
Because the cold fact is that there is no resurrection without death.
'Unless a grain of wheat falls into the earth and dies, it remains alone;
but if it dies, it bears much fruit' (John 12:24).

I have said that healing in Christianity is a process of death and
resurrection in which man, anguished in his existential separation
from Christ and from other men and from the cosmos, is once more
united with the one he loves and for whom he longs. In Buddhism
there is a similar pattern. It is precisely because the self cuts man
off from the whole that it must die; and it is by death and the loss of
self that man enters into *nirvana* or union with the cosmos. A friend
of mine, a Catholic priest, who practised some Zen told me that the
Zen master once said to him with some severity, 'God sent his only
Son into the world to die. And you must die too. So die!' This is one
more example of Buddhist ability to see the relevance of Christian
dogma for daily living. How well he saw that as Christ died, his
followers must die too if they are to enter into resurrection.

Buddhism, then, sees the necessity of death and of radical detachment as the gateway to *nirvana*. While I would not equate *nirvana*
and resurrection (that would be an unpardonable oversimplification),
I do believe that both concepts are striving to answer man's most
terrible and most basic question – how to be healed from the anguish
of separation and loneliness and isolation and death. In both religions
death is conquered because it is the gateway to something else.
Perhaps *resurrection* is a clearer affirmation of something hinted at by
nirvana.

And in both religions, prior to death there is the inevitable detachment. In Buddhism, as we have seen, selfish desire builds up the
illusory ego and magnifies the gap that separates man from the all.
That is why one must reject all desire and all clinging, not only to
the comforts and luxuries and pleasures of life but also to knowledge
and the process of thinking. The most rigorous detachment is
demanded in the very practice of Zen; because one is constantly

renouncing one's natural desire for conceptual knowledge. And the process in Christian meditation is rather similar. 'Whoever of you does not renounce all that he has cannot be my disciple' (Luke 14:33). And here 'all' means all. St John of the Cross demands detachment, never from God, it is true, but from thoughts and ideas and feelings of God. The justification for this is scriptural. God is above everything – ideas, idols, images and words of all kinds. Man's perennial temptation (as was Israel's) has always been to put God in a box or in a category and thus to be in control. Conceptual knowledge is a way of mastery that must be abandoned in favour of a non-conceptual knowledge, a whole new mode of knowing and loving which goes into the silence of the cloud or the dark night.

So we end with an awful paradox. From the viewpoint of science and common sense, sickness and death are the great evils to be conquered. And here we find religions claiming that they are conditions for true healing and that they lead to life. The practical conclusion is that sickness and death *are* great evils and that with the scientist we alleviate suffering; we fight death; we try to prolong life. We use medicine and biofeedback and even meditation in a relentless war against the great enemies, which are suffering and death. But when we have made the maximum human effort to ward off pain and postpone the end – only at this point are we justified in saying that death is swallowed up in victory. 'O death, where is thy sting?' (1 Corinthians 15:55) Through death comes resurrection and the deeper healing.

12. *Cosmic healing*

We live in an age of planetization. That is to say, we live in an age when man longs to be liberated from the confining narrowness of nationalism in order to build the earth. Seeing the place of our little planet in the complex totality of the infinite universe, modern man thinks more and more in cosmic terms and aspires to act in a cosmic way. I was impressed to read how the astronauts, looking back on the earth from outer space, came to a new awareness of things. It is even said that several of them, detached from the earth and its little problems, underwent a change of consciousness resembling a mystical experience. This is highly significant. May it not be part of our movement towards a new cosmology and a new consciousness?

If the meditation discussed in this book holds an appeal for contemporary people, this is to some extent because of its cosmic implications. In an earlier chapter I said that the Zen master 'sits' for the universe. This is not, I believe, just pious talk. It has a basis in psychology and even, perhaps, in physics. Because meditation entails an expansion of mind, a loss of self, an entrance into altered states of consciousness, a thrust into a dimension beyond time and space, in such wise that not only man's spirit but his very psyche and body become somehow cosmic. I have already spoken at length about the impact of meditation on the body, and I will not repeat it here. Only let me add that every religious tradition has stories of out-of-the-body experiences, of saints knowing intuitively what is happening in other parts of the world, of the impact of prayer on distant people, and so on. And while a good deal of this may well be legend, I doubt if we can dismiss the whole thing out of hand. There is in the human body a cosmic mystery that we will never fathom.

How modern physics would attempt to explain the cosmic dimension of the body I do not know. Everyone will admit that the whole question is exceedingly complex since we do not know what matter is, what the body is, what energy is. But one thing becomes increasingly clear: that the universe is so unified that every movement or action, however slight, has its repercussions throughout the whole. And man is part of this network. At one time he thought he could extricate himself from the totality to view the universe objectively as a serene and detached outsider. Now we know this cannot be. Receiving influence from every corner of the mysterious universe, he likewise influences it; and his actions are like the proverbial pebble thrown into the pond and causing endless ripples. I myself believe that next to God the most influential person in the cosmos is the mystic.

In Eastern meditation the body is prepared for its cosmic role by the emphasis on posture. One comes to a new sense of one's body and of its links with the universe. This is done more especially through attention to the breath. For in the oriental tradition, this breath is not just the air that fills my lungs, giving energy to my little body. Rather is it the breath of the universe. Through breathing I arrive at a harmony with the vibrating cosmos. Similar to this in the Western tradition is the breath or the wind or the *spiratio*, which speaks of the Holy Spirit breathing in me, uniting me to all men and to all creation and to the Father. This, in the New Testament, is 'the Spirit of Jesus'.

St Paul is well aware of the cosmic dimensions of the body, particularly of the resurrected body. For him the great prototype of man become cosmic is Christ in his glory. The body of Christ comes first, for he is 'the first-born' (Colossians 1:18), and after it, and in him, all the saved become cosmic too. Christ is Son by nature: we are sons by grace. But when asked what the resurrected and cosmic body looks like, Paul answers almost abruptly: 'Don't ask foolish questions!' He has been talking about the certainty of resurrection in Christ, and then he goes on: 'But some one will ask, "How are the dead raised? With what kind of body do they come?" You foolish man! What you sow does not come to life unless it dies ...' (1 Corinthians 15:35–36). And then Paul goes on to say that there are many kinds of bodies, many kinds of flesh (how modern indeed!), and that there is a whole dimension of matter that we simply cannot understand. 'For not all flesh is alike, but there is one kind for men, another for animals, another for birds, and another for fish. There are celestial bodies and there are terrestrial bodies ... star differs from star in glory' (1 Corinthians 15:39–41). 'Not all flesh is alike'! The bodies of the dead are with us in their resurrected form but they are in a new cosmic dimension which baffles our powers of imagination and intelligence. Yet for Paul this movement towards cosmification (if I may coin a word) begins at baptism, continues all through life in a movement from flesh to spirit, and reaches its culminating point through death. Now, no longer possessing a fleshly body, man has become a 'spiritual body'.

Nor is all this empty theory. In Japan, thanks to the Christian dialogue with Zen, some Christians are exploring forms of meditation that will bring the meditator to an experience of the cosmic body of Christ through a sense of his own body. To the Catholic Christian the notion of the universal body of Christ is already familiar because of his belief in the eucharistic presence of Christ transfiguring the world. And he believes that this presence is the risen body of Christ within his body, transforming it and making it cosmic. What is exciting about the whole thing is that this body of Christ which lives within him is united with the poor and the sick and the suffering and with the whole human race. It is also united with the Father, of whom Jesus could say, 'I and the Father are one' (John 10:30). Such is the cosmic destiny of man – union with Christ, union with the Father, union with man and the universe.

In the above I may have digressed too much from the main point of this chapter, which was not to speak about the cosmic dimension of meditation but about certain people who, realizing their cosmic role, play a great part in the healing of the universe.

For the universe itself is sick. I have spoken about healing of body, healing of mind, and the deeper healing enacted at the level of being. But all the sickness here involved is linked to an even more fundamental sickness which is that of the universe itself. We have already seen the clear-cut Buddhist stand on this point. Paul, too, in Romans paints a fine picture of a universe sick and groaning as it waits for the promised deliverance:

> For the creation was subjected to futility, not of its own will but by the will of him who subjected it in hope; because the creation itself will be set free from its bondage to decay and obtain the glorious liberty of the children of God. We know that the whole creation has been groaning in travail together until now; and not only the creation, but we ourselves, who have the first fruits of the Spirit, groan inwardly as we wait for adoption as sons, the redemption of our bodies.   (Romans 8:20–23)

Here is a universe labouring in the pains of childbirth, unfinished, incomplete, contingent. Just as the great suffering of the mystic is his sense of separation from his end, which is the resurrection; so the great suffering of the universe is its separation from the end towards which it is straining and striving.

The sickness of the cosmos is due to a variety of causes. There is the fact of contingency, the fact of incompleteness and unfinished evolution, together with the anguished groaning that necessarily accompanies parturition. There is the inevitable failure and waste that goes along with growth. Then there is the evil arising from man's refusal to build the earth, from the glorification of his ego, from his refusal to love – and, even more terrible, from his perversion of love. And there is the activity of one who put the earth in bondage. All this makes the very universe itself shout out with Paul: 'Who will deliver me from this body of death?' (Romans 7:24)

Yet the healing of the cosmos is not automatic or inevitable. It will only be healed through man.

And here lies the vocation of the cosmic person who takes on himself the totality of things and even the totality of suffering. Here lies the vocation of the mystic. The Zen master 'sitting' for the universe is in a logical position, since in Buddhism the small individual self is illusory and does not really exist. The only ego that can be purified is the ego of the universe and this is purified in him. In a somewhat different way, the notion of one person healing the nation and the universe is dramatically portrayed in Isaiah:

> Surely he has borne our griefs
>   and carried our sorrows;
> yet we esteemed him stricken,
>   smitten by God, and afflicted.
> But he was wounded for our transgressions,
>   he was bruised for our iniquities;
> upon him was the chastisement that made us whole,
>   and with his stripes we are healed.
> All we like sheep have gone astray;
>   we have turned every one to his own way;
> and the Lord has laid on him
>   the iniquity of us all.   (Isaiah 53:4–6)

Here one man suffers for the people. The cosmos is purified in him. This way of thinking is central to the New Testament, whose authors create a whole Christology from this servant of Yahweh in Isaiah. For them Jesus in Gethsemane and on the cross is this cosmic man who takes the woes of the world on his shoulders, who suffers not for himself (for he is sinless) but for man and the universe.

And the mystics follow after Jesus in that they become ever more universal. Paul is aware that his suffering is cosmic and can heal the broken totality of things: 'Now I rejoice in my sufferings for your sake, and in my flesh I complete what is lacking in Christ's afflictions for the sake of his body, that is, the church' (Colossians 1:24). Nor is it only Paul. Any Christian who sincerely meditates is becoming one with the universal Christ in a process that reaches its climax in resurrection, the ultimate universalization of man. Yet this is full of paradox in that the further one enters the thicket of the joyful and ecstatic mystical life the greater becomes one's capacity for suffering – a suffering that is redemptive.

If it be asked, however, why suffering heals the universe, I would answer that in itself it heals nothing. What heals is love, which is most dramatically expressed in suffering. Love is the highest form of human energy; and in an earlier chapter I have already spoken of its incredible power to heal. This holds true in the cosmic dimension also. The universe is healed by men and women of universal love. It is not, I believe, the achievements of science themselves that build the cosmos, but the love for humanity that underlies them. And the same holds true for suffering – it is not the suffering itself that matters but the love that underlies it. The love that builds the cosmos is universal love, the highest love that can fill the human heart.

Though the working of mystical love and its power to heal are mysteries that no man understands, I would like to hazard a few remarks that may throw light on this cosmic adventure of the mystics.

First of all let me say that all knowledge and love open us up to new areas of experience by which we live in others and are necessarily affected by their joys and sufferings. Was it not Socrates who spoke of the inexpressible bliss of deep and dreamless sleep? Total ignorance, he realized, is a form of bliss, whereas to know and to love is to expose oneself to the beautiful possibility of joy and the awful possibility of sorrow.

Now this is particularly true of mystical knowledge and love. For this goes beyond images and concepts to a deeper level of awareness wherein we are one with the person we love. Here is a knowledge of identity, of empathy, of indwelling. And when it gets really deep we become part of others to such an extent that what happens to them happens to us – their joy becomes our joy, their sorrow becomes our sorrow. So the mystic, who loves all men with a universal love and who lives in all men, rejoices with those who rejoice and weeps with those who weep. This was the case with great-souled mystics like Paul himself or Pope John or Dag Hammarskjöld or Gandhi. These were people who by reason of their greatness loved more, rejoiced more and suffered more. Their very universality gave them greater capacity for joy and greater capacity for suffering. One is reminded of the great Bodhisattva who feels so deeply the suffering of the tiniest living thing that he refuses to enter *nirvana* until every sentient being is saved. And so he remains outside until the end of time.

And the Christian mystic who knows and loves the cosmic Christ takes on himself the joy and the suffering of the cosmos. His love, like Paul's, makes him live in Christ and Christ in him. But the Christ with whom he is now so deeply involved is the total Christ who suffers in the wars and pestilence and social injustices that afflict mankind. Opening his heart to the cosmic Christ, the mystic opens his heart to the joys and sufferings of everybody as well as to the vast universe; for his beloved is 'the mountains, the solitary wooded valleys, strange islands . . . silent music'. All this dwells within him in its ecstasy and its agony. That is why the suffering servant in Isaiah is wounded for our sins and bruised for our iniquities.

And his love heals precisely because it makes him mystically present to all, precisely because through indwelling he can take upon himself everyone's burdens. His love heals just as a mother heals her child or as the lover heals the beloved. In the same way the universal love of the mystic helps heal the cosmos and man, in whom the cosmos comes to full flowering.

As for the goal of the cosmic healing process, I believe it is best understood in an evolutionary context. Surveying the vast stream of evolution, now led forward by the human spearhead, Teilhard asks where it is going. As a scientist and a man of faith, he cannot envisage such a process without an end or goal or point of convergence. If no such end exists, he declares, the human effort is value-less. If it does exist, it is personal, since the evolution of the universe is more and more in the direction of personalization. And so he comes to affirm the existence of Omega, the point of convergence, the Prime Mover ahead. But while Aristotle's Prime Mover was a thinking being ('the thought that thinks itself'), the Teilhardian Prime Mover ahead is a loving personal centre of attraction. Omega is at once transcendent, like a huge magnet that pulls the universe to itself, and at the same time immanently present to the universe which it propels towards its end. Omega stands at the apex of things like a lover luring to himself his beloved who is the totality of creation.

Besides being a scientist, Teilhard was a Christian. That is why he sees Omega as the risen Christ, while the point of convergence is the *pleroma* or fullness of time, the completion of God's plan 'to unite all things in him, things in heaven and things on earth' (Ephesians 1:10). Such is the Christology around which Teilhard's thought revolves. He sees ahead the Christ who said, 'I, when I am lifted up from the earth, will draw all men to myself' (John 12:32). Drawing all men to himself, he is the point on which a world in evolution finally converges. This is the Son of Man who will come in the clouds of glory; this is the Christ of whom Paul writes, 'Who shall separate us from the love of Christ?' (Romans 8:35) If Christ is the Prime Mover ahead, drawing all things to himself, then it becomes literally true that nothing can separate us from the magnetic power of his love, which penetrates the whole. Omega, then, is personalized love, the *agape* of the scriptures. Omega is the divine milieu.

How cosmic is the experience of one who loves 'the mountains, the solitary wooded valleys, strange islands . . . silent music'! His is a love affair with the universe. And like every true love affair it is healing and strengthening and beautiful. It is through such love that the universe will be transfigured.

INTIMACY

13. *Meditation and intimacy*

The modern world shows great interest in anything that concerns community and interpersonal relations. Perhaps we are beginning to see that if we are to live in harmony on this crowded planet we had better find some formula for community living – and pretty quickly. Teilhard put it well when he said that it used to be 'Love one another if you want to be perfect', but now it is 'Love one another if you want to survive'. If we are to get on with the business of planet-ization and building the earth, we must learn how to live together. Hence our interest in communal living, interpersonal relations, group encounters, sensitivity training, and all the rest. It seems that community is one of the great preoccupations of our day.

And related to this is the modern interest in intimacy. New views on marriage stress the dimension of intimacy between husband and wife. New thinking on religious celibacy stresses personal love and intimacy in the single state. It seems that man has reached a stage in evolution where intimacy is not only one of his top priorities but also a psychological necessity of life.

In spite of all the talk about intimacy, however, there is little agreement about what the word means. Sometimes it is equated with sincerity in human relations, or with frankness and openness. Or it is put as the opposite of playing games. But what interests me here is that not infrequently deep interpersonal relations and intimacy are associated with profundity in meditation. Centres for sensitivity training and the development of human potential often hold courses both in encounter and in meditation, as though they instinctively felt that these two things are somehow related. And here I want to ask how, and to what extent, they are in fact related.

Faced with this question, I can immediately see two reasons why meditation might lead people to know and love one another at a deeper level of awareness. One is the non-attachment that necessarily accompanies the meditational process. The other is the empathetic knowledge already discussed in the last chapter. Let me say a word about these two points. And first about non-attachment.

Modern psychology reminds us that to be truly intimate we must not cling to people. We must let them be, leaving them the liberty to be themselves, to lead their own lives, to make their own decisions, to choose their own beliefs, to follow the spirit within them. The fact is, of course, that most of us cannot do this. We cling to those we love, trying to make them what we want them to be and to mould them according to our plans. This destroys union and intimacy.

It would be relatively easy to abandon our clinging fixations if they were in the conscious mind. But more often they are not. They are lurking in those nebulous, subliminal depths which are outside our control and even beyond the fringe of awareness. Sometimes we can only guess at their existence from the inexplicable anguish that crosses the mind in certain relationships. Often such relationships are partly projections: we are superimposing our father or mother images upon others, clinging to others as a child clings to its parents. Or a mother will project into her child her own unconscious frustrations, forcing him to lead the life she wanted to live but could not. Needless to say, she is not aware of this; in her own eyes she is the loving mother. But she cannot be intimate with this child because she loves herself in him.

Depth can only be achieved when we get beyond projections to the core of the other's personality – that is to say, when person meets person. And this, in turn, can only be done when I am detached from my own subliminal imagery, self-centred desires, unconscious frustrations, childish projections, and all the rest. In other words, a first condition for intimacy is the purification of the conscious and unconscious mind.

Put in terms of the transactional analysis mentioned earlier in this book, intimacy, I believe, can only be achieved when a relationship is purified of excessive influence from Parent and Child. As long as the Child in me constantly relates to the Parent in someone else, the chances for intimacy are slim because the relationship is distorted by the interference of half-buried memories and voices from the past. If I am to meet the core of the other at the core of my own being I must 'let go' of the neurotic Child and the finger-wagging Parent. And again this would be easily done if these phantoms were only in the conscious mind. But often they are not. They are lodged in subliminal areas, so that we cannot analyse the transaction even when we want to do so. Once more, purification of the unconscious is demanded. Only when this is done can person meet person without playing games. Only then does it become possible for adult to meet adult or, even more wonderful, for natural Child to meet natural Child. Only then is the stage set for a meeting that can be a real mystical experience. Detachment from one's internal states and purification from all clinging are the inexorable conditions for such mystical encounter.

Now vertical meditation that goes beyond thoughts and images to the inner core of silence is the arch-enemy of conscious and unconscious clinging. This is particularly true in Buddhist *samadhi*, with its emphasis on silence, nothingness, emptiness, the void and the cessation of desire. Buddhism declares (and how truly!) that clinging causes illusion, blinding us to the true nature of reality and making us live in a phantasmal world of ghosts. And so, in the silence of a meditation that penetrates through layer after layer of consciousness, it liberates man from the tyranny of his internal fixations. It penetrates those murky subliminal depths and cleans them up. And then, liberated from clinging and possessiveness, I can see and relate to the other as other. No longer my idea of the other but the other as he is in himself. No longer my idea of myself but my true, deep and authentic self. Now I am free to love and receive love. Furthermore (and this is a characteristic of all contemplative experience) I become habitually present and open to the here-and-now. Conceptual ideas *about* persons and things withdraw us from the reality that lies before our eyes, bringing us into the past. The intuitive, non-attached person, on the other hand, is a now-person. He sees the other as he is today, not as he was yesterday. The discipline of detachment has led him to a continual freshness of perception (remember how this even appeared in the 'click experiments' of Dr Hirai!) which makes possible a deeper authenticity and gift of oneself.

This non-attachment, so characteristic of Buddhism, is found in all those forms of vertical meditation that use the *mantra*, the *koan*, the *mandala*, or just imageless silence. It is found pre-eminently in Christian contemplation. The meditational process clears the upper layers of the mind, opening up the unconscious, going beyond fixations to deeper layers of psychic life, thus bringing the meditator to an inner liberty in which he is freed from the tyranny of his own interior states, whether these be his Parent, his Child, or his inordinate desires. And all this is preparation for the phenomenon that we call intimacy.

Yet non-attachment, however valuable, does not constitute the essence of intimacy. It is no more than a condition, a preparation, a liberation. Indeed, as we have seen earlier, non-attachment in itself could be a condition for hatred and destruction: it could free the meditator to do evil with equanimity. Much more important is the second point I mentioned; namely, the knowledge of empathy, which forms the very core of religious meditation whether Buddhist or Christian. This is the knowledge that goes beyond thoughts and images and concepts. It springs from love and compassion, and it leads to indwelling. It is the knowledge and love of a Paul who discovers that he lives in Christ and that Christ lives in him. Paul keeps saying that he is 'in Christ' and he also experiences that Christ is in him. The faithful, too, are 'in Christ', and he prays that Christ may be in them – 'that Christ may dwell in your hearts through faith' (Ephesians 3:17). Here is the very centre of intimacy and indwelling. And something like the Pauline intimacy with Jesus can be found in a relationship between close friends who know and love one another at a deep level of awareness. In the *Introduction to the Devout Life*, Francis de Sales quotes the words of St Gregory of Nazianzen about his remarkable friendship with St Basil:

> It seemed as though there were but one soul between us, having two bodies. And if we must not believe those who say that all things are in all things, yet you must believe this, that we were both in each one of us, and the one in the other . . .
>
> (Francis de Sales, ch. 18)

These two men were mystics. They had experienced non-attachment and meditational states of consciousness so that their friendship culminated in an indwelling that reminds one of Paul's friendship with Christ. And the essence of such intimacy is a personal love, liberated through non-attachment, whereby two people meet at the core of their being in an ecstatic encounter.

I like to stress the role of empathy and love because it has been suggested in encounter groups that the psychological process alone can effect intimacy. As though the very fact of meditating, entering into deeper states of awareness and expanding one's consciousness, would effect intimacy without the religious dimension of faith and love. I do not believe that this is so. I do not believe that any psychological process, divorced from faith and love and commitment, can produce intimacy and indwelling. This was brought home to me on reading of some laboratory experiments performed in the field of secular or non-religious meditation. These experiments resulted not in indwelling but in *merging*. Let me describe them briefly.

In one experiment, subjects are asked to meditate by gazing for long periods at an object such as a blue vase. As they stare and as their meditation deepens, some of them experience the sensation of merging with the vase and of becoming one with it. Or they feel that the vase is inside them. Here is a report from one researcher:

> Merging was reported by subject A, who from the very beginning reported striking alterations in her perception of the vase and her relation to it. She reported, 'One of the points that I remember most vividly is when I really began to feel, you know, almost as though the blue and I were perhaps merging, or that vase and I were. I almost got scared to the point where I found myself bringing myself back in some way from it . . . It was as though everything was sort of merging and I was somehow losing my sense of consciousness almost.' This merging experience was characteristic of all of this subject's meditation sessions, but she soon became familiar with it and ceased to describe it as anything remarkable. Following the sixth session she reported, 'At one point it felt . . . as though the vase were in my head rather than out there; I knew it was out there but it seemed as though it were almost a part of me.' 'I think that I almost felt at that moment as though, you know, the image is really in me, it's not out there.'
>
> (Tart, p. 206)

In addition to merging with the vase, subjects reported that they became personally attached to it: they felt disappointed when it was taken away or if it was missing when they entered the room. In other words, prolonged meditation had developed within them some kind of love for, and union with, the vase.

Merging with a vase or a flower is one thing: merging with a person is quite another. Here, too, laboratory experiments give us food for thought. After a series of sessions in mutual hypnosis, where two subjects, Bill and Anne, hypnotized one another, Dr Tart of the University of California at Davis made the following observation:

> The alteration that most impressed (and later frightened) the subjects, however, was the feeling of *merging* with each other at

times, especially in the final mutual hypnosis session. This seemed
like a partial fusion of identities, a partial loss of the distinction
between I and Thou. This was felt to be good at the time, but
later the subjects perceived this as a threat to their individual
autonomy.   (Tart, p. 306)

Dr Tart himself is not convinced that this merging is always
emotionally helpful, and he goes on:

A . . . possible danger to be mentioned is that the 'forced' intimacy
produced by this technique may be unsettling . . . Our culture
does not prepare people for sudden, intense intimacy. I know of a
roughly comparable case of two married couples who took LSD-25
together; each experienced an intense merging of identities with
the three others. Because of the sudden and unexpected intensity
of these feelings the couples had a great deal of difficulty in their
emotional relationships to each other for several months afterwards,
all centered around feelings that they had seen too much of each
other's real selves, more than their previous relationship had
prepared them to handle comfortably.   (Tart, p. 307)

In the mutual hypnosis sessions, Dr Tart tells us, Anne was
willing to continue; but one sympathizes with Bill who was strongly
opposed to any further exploration and subsequently lost interest in
the whole business.

Finally let me quote yet another researcher in meditation and
consciousness, who suggests the following path to intimacy:

Place yourself face to face with another person. Look at him and
be aware when your mind wanders. Be aware when you treat his
face like an object, a design, or play perceptual games with it.
Distortions may appear which tell you what you project into the
relationship: angels, devils, animals and all the human possibilities
may appear in his face. Eventually you may move past these visual
fantasies into the genuine presence of another human being.
                                                             (Tart, p. 186)

I have quoted the above experiments because I believe they shed
some light on the reality which we call intimacy; and in them the
strength and weakness of the scientific approach is evident.

In the deepest intimacy, it seems to me, there is no merging; but there is indwelling, to such an extent that people can live in one another and be part of one another even when separated by thousands of miles. What makes the difference between merging and indwelling is, I believe, personal love and commitment and trust. Two people can enter into deeply altered states of consciousness either through drugs or hypnosis, or even by the practice of non-attachment, and they can float into one another's psyche with a terrifying loss of identity. But where there is no love and trust, what human value can this possibly have? And where love and trust are lacking, how terrible can be this 'forced' intimacy! Furthermore, love and trust must grow; and ordinarily this takes time. I cannot believe that we can blandly walk into the core of another's being by altering our consciousness with drugs or hypnosis or other techniques. Nor can we do so by staring for hours at another's face, unless our love and trust correspond to the length of our gaze. It must be awful to be stared at for hours by someone who does not love you; and it must be awful to stare for hours at someone we do not love. All this is so different from the ecstatic love affair in which the beloved is 'the mountains, the solitary wooded valleys, strange islands . . . silent music'. Without the mystical dimension of love and trust, meditation runs the risk of inhumanity and mechanical manipulation.

Obviously this is not meant to be a blanket criticism of scientific research in the area of meditation. All I want to say is that science needs the complementarity of religion if it is to be really human in this field.

To understand indwelling, as opposed to merging, it is helpful once again to recall the Teilhardian principal that union in the personal differentiates. When people meet at the level of personal love achieved through radical non-attachment, they do not merge; nor are they absorbed in one another; nor do they lose their identity. On the contrary, it is precisely in their union with the other that they find their true selves. There is at once a total unity and a total alterity.

Such intimacy and such indwelling is a central theme of the fourth gospel. 'Abide in me, and I in you', says Jesus (John 15:4). And he prays that his disciples may be one, that they may be totally one, that they may be completely one (John 17:21–23). And yet they are not one, because each retains his autonomous personality. 'In that day you will know that I am in my Father, and you in me, and I in you' (John 14:20). The model of intimacy is the union of the Father and the Son who are totally one God while remaining distinct, personal and autonomous. Paradox here reaches its climax. Yet I believe that hidden in these chapters of the fourth gospel are some of the greatest insights the world has ever heard. For here we have the notion of person – so central to any doctrine of intimacy – of the inviolability and uniqueness of the divine person and the human person, linked to the notion of total union. Never, never can the man or woman who has been called by name be lost in an amorphous mass of unified nothingness. On the contrary, the greater the union the more autonomous and free becomes the person. The impulse towards unity that characterizes all love results not in merging, not in absorption, but in a luminous presence of person to person.

This intimacy, however, is bought at a high price. Non-attachment is a painful process in which the deep caverns of the psyche are purified from jealousy, hatred, possessiveness, anger and selfishness. Without this purification, husband and wife, parent and child, friend and friend can never be intimate. But (and this is the beautiful doctrine of the Christian mystics) it is love which purifies and detaches. The process is like that of the man who joyfully sold everything for love of the treasure hidden in the field (Matthew 13:44). In our case the treasure is the deep core of the other, the mystery of his or her personality. It is this that we love; and our search for this treasure demands the renunciation of lesser goods.

Realizing that love detaches, we can see how the quest for intimacy can be filled with joy and filled with pain. With joy because love is a joyful business, and who is more ecstatic than the lover? With pain because (in the words of D. H. Lawrence) 'Love is the great Asker'. It is always asking us to leave the lesser for the greater; it is always asking us to leave the rind to reach the core; it is always asking us to go on and on in perpetual exploration. And in the last analysis intimacy is less a *thing* than an *event* or a happening. That is why it defies analysis and escapes definition. It can never be circumscribed. 'The mountains, the solitary wooded valleys, strange islands . . . silent music.'

14. *Mystical friendship*

Earlier in this book I said that meditation opens up levels of psychic life that are ordinarily dormant. St Teresa calls these deeper levels of awareness 'interior senses' and she speaks of a seeing, hearing, touching and embracing that are different from the seeing, hearing, touching and embracing that we associate with external sensation. A sixteenth-century Spaniard, Teresa used vivid and dramatic language to speak of a phenomenon which other mystics describe in simpler terms. They talk of relishing and savouring the deeper realities, while Bergson speaks of 'deep, creative emotion'. All are striving to describe a dimension of psychic life which most of us rarely actuate because we live at a superficial level of awareness.

In the case of Teresa these mystical faculties are operative chiefly in her relationship with Christ. It is Christ that she sees and hears and loves with the most profound faculties of her psyche. But (and this is the point I wish to make here) these same faculties can also be brought into play in human relationships. This was the case with the mystics. Their most intimate interpersonal relations were the outcome and extension of their profound contemplative experience. That is why in dealing with their fellow-men they could see and hear and touch at a new level. That is why they could sometimes read hearts and know intuitively what others were thinking. I am not speaking here about extrasensory perception but about a certain mystical awareness, an intuitive knowledge, a deep feeling. No superficial emotion this, but an extraordinary empathy. When two mystics were friends (and often they were) there arose between them a remarkable indwelling which enabled them to say one to the other: 'As the Father has loved me, so have I loved you; abide in my love' (John 15:9).

One of the most attractive writers on the subject of mystical friendship is the twelfth-century Cistercian, Aelred of Rievaulx. Living in a religious culture which set great store on the beauty of friendship, he composed a little *Treatise on Spiritual Friendship* in which, like many of his contemporaries, he makes extensive and mystical use of the Song of Solomon. 'O that you would kiss me with the kisses of your mouth!' (Song of Solomon 1:2) Aelred comments that a kiss can be exchanged at levels of consciousness transcending the physical. Just as Teresa speaks of a seeing that goes beyond the physical seeing with the eyes of the body, so Aelred speaks of a kiss that goes beyond all physical kissing with the lips of the body. Such a kiss is, in fact, nothing other than a meeting of two spirits. 'In a kiss', he writes, 'two spirits meet, mingle, and become one; and as a result, there arises in the mind a wonderful feeling of delight that awakens and binds together the love of them that kiss' (Aelred, p. 673).

Following a contemporary custom which looked on perfection as a ladder rising up towards the spiritualization of matter (the Pauline movement from flesh to spirit), he divides the kiss into three ascending stages of consciousness or awareness. According to the different kinds of union 'there is a kiss of the body, a kiss of the spirit and a kiss of the mind. The kiss of the body is made by the impress of the lips; the kiss of the spirit by the union of hearts; the kiss of the mind by the infusion of grace into the soul through the Spirit of God' (Aelred, ibid.). Then he describes three types of union, beginning with the bodily kiss:

> Hence the bodily kiss is not to be given or accepted except for certain and just reasons; for example, as a sign of reconciliation when enemies become friends. Or it may be given as a sign of peace, as those who are about to receive Holy Communion in church express interior peace by an exterior kiss. It may be given as a sign of love, as between bride and bridegroom; or as it is given and received by friends after a long separation. It can be given as a sign of Catholic unity, as is done when one welcomes a guest. But just as many people, for the purpose of indulging their sensuality or cruelty, misuse water, fire, iron, food and air, all of which are good in themselves, so also perverse and low-minded men endeavour to conceal their crimes even with this good gesture which the natural law established to express the affections we have described. (Aelred, ibid.)

After this sound advice about the bodily kiss, Aelred goes on to speak about the kiss of the spirit, exchanged between friends. This is a meeting of minds and an ecstasy of spirit. Going beyond anything bodily, it is an act of the most intense intimacy, bringing in its train overflowing joy:

The kiss of the spirit is the special prerogative of friends who are bound by a covenant of friendship. It is given and received not by the touching of the mouth but by the union of hearts, not by the union of lips but by the mingling of spirits. Here the Spirit of God makes everything chaste, and by his participation infuses a celestial relish. This kiss I call the kiss of Christ, which however he does not give by his own mouth, but by the mouth of another. For in the two friends he creates such a sacred emotion that they feel as if they are two souls in one body, and they say with the prophet: 'Behold how good and pleasant it is for brethren to dwell together as one.'   (Aelred, ibid.)

In an earlier chapter of this book I spoke of a communal *samadhi* or prayer of quiet that can exist between people who love one another deeply. It is easy to see how such union could rise to moments of intense intimacy such as those of which Aelred speaks. For here in moments of ecstatic indwelling and enlightenment the friends become one while remaining themselves.

In the above stage, the risen Christ is present since he is at the core of the two persons who meet and in him they are united. But Aelred's third stage goes on even further to a meeting with Christ himself. This, it is interesting to note, is only achieved after rigorous purification, 'when all earthly affections have been mastered and when all earthly desires have been lulled to sleep'. Here are his words:

When, therefore, the mind has become accustomed to this kiss and recognizes that all this sweetness comes from Christ it says as if musing to itself: 'Oh, if only he himself would come.' And with this it aspires to the kiss of the mind, and cries out with ardent desire, 'Let him kiss me with the kiss of his mouth.' So when all earthly affections have been mastered and when all earthly desires have been lulled to sleep, the mind finds delight in the kiss of only Christ, rests in his embrace, exulting and saying: 'His left hand is under my head; his right hand shall embrace me.'   (Aelred, ibid.)

Aelred, then, sees friendship as a way to Christ. One is reminded of the Chinese *tao* and the Hindu *ways* that lead to enlightenment. Aelred here adds another way, a beautiful way and one that is totally in harmony with, or an expression of, the gospel; namely, the way of friendship. Obviously this is not a way to Christ divorced from his members, as though one jettisoned human friendship when one reached the goal. Rather is it a discovery of the true personality of the friend while Christ is present as a third partner in their love.

Writing in the Hellenistic tradition, Aelred borrows freely from Cicero who, in turn, is rooted in Aristotle. But beneath the veneer of Hellenism his real inspiration comes from the Bible and its story of the Covenant. Let me say a word about this here.

The thunder and flashing lightning of Sinai herald a new era in interpersonal relations, as Moses wends his way up the mountain, enters the cloud of unknowing and speaks to Yahweh face to face as a man might speak to his friend. Here is the grand seal on a divine intimacy which goes back to Abraham and even to the early chapters of Genesis. Moses, the friend of Yahweh, now mediates a covenant which is nothing less than a marriage between the bride and the bridegroom, a bond of friendship between Israel and Yahweh, a link between man and God. It is the archetype and model of human marriage and of any other friendship, such as that between David and Jonathan, who made a solemn covenant because each loved the other 'as his own soul' (1 Samuel 18:3). And what a friendship that was! What pathos echoes through David's dirge for the dead Jonathan:

> I am distressed for you, my brother Jonathan;
> very pleasant have you been to me;
> your love to me was wonderful,
> passing the love of women.

> (2 Samuel 1:26)

And the love of David and Jonathan is an integral part of their love for Yahweh and their role in salvation history.

Ideally speaking, friendship partakes of the characteristics of the Covenant. It is a deep commitment to another person, reaching its peak-point in a readiness to die: 'Greater love has no man than this, that a man lay down his life for his friends' (John 15:13). It is a mutual commitment: I love you, and you return my love, just as the New Covenant will say, 'We love [God], because he first loved us' (1 John 4:19). Again, it is a free commitment and the Bible stresses that covenant love can never be forced. What pathos fills the words of Revelation: 'Behold, I stand at the door and knock; if any one hears my voice and opens the door, I will come in to him and eat with him, and he with me' (Revelation 3:20). Here we strike the note of freedom. We can knock all day on someone's door; Christ himself can knock all day on someone's door; but if the other chooses to keep that door closed, no one can enter. We are free to accept or reject friendship. I can draft all the covenants I like, but if the other does not respond I am powerless. Yahweh himself cannot – because he will not – break into the heart of a man who is reluctant to open. Friendship is a meeting of persons who dwell in one another as Jesus dwells in the Father and the Father in him. Finally, the partners in the covenant must be faithful, just as Yahweh is faithful to his people, even when they desert him to play the harlot in Egypt. The steadfast love of Yahweh is the supreme model of human fidelity.

And the friendship of Aelred is based on this covenant. What makes it peculiarly mystical is the intuitive depth at which it is enacted in Christ. Going beyond thoughts and concepts and images to reach the inner core of another, it creates a bond, a mutual fidelity, a union in Christ that ordinary friendship does not know.

Aelred wrote for, and about, his fellow monks. But the doctrine he evolved is capable of much broader application. It is even relevant in the turbulent area of man-woman relationships which become more and more critical in the cultural revolution that characterizes our day. With institutional marriage in process of transformation, with all kinds of experiments (wise and otherwise) being attempted, with the increasing desire of married couples to be friends and intimates, not just sexual partners – in this environment, Aelred may have a message for modern man and modern woman. The presupposition is that they are open to mysticism through love and faith and meditation and non-attachment. For this will develop their interior senses, leading them through those stages that culminate in the kiss of Christ, a situation where Christ is somehow present in their love as the Spirit is present in the love of the Father for the Son. And sexual intercourse, being an expression of, and way to, this deeper union of mind and heart, becomes fully human and spiritually creative.

For meditation in all the great religions leads to remarkable control of sexuality. Not that sexual power diminishes with depth in meditation. On the contrary, the non-attachment that accompanies such depth penetrates to the subliminal caverns of psychic life, liberating men and women from the unconscious fears and traumatic anxieties that sometimes cause impotence, frigidity, lack of pleasure and reluctance to give oneself physically to another. In this sense, meditation, far from weakening, may liberate one's sexual energy; and this is one of the claims of Yoga. But together with this liberation comes a power and a self-mastery (and this is chastity) which enables people to express their love sexually when it is appropriate to do so and to refrain from physical expression when circumstances so demand. And to do so in such a way that their love, rooted at the deep core of their being, never grows cold. Though Aelred had nothing like this in mind, his principles might well lead to a mysticism of marriage.

Yet another area in which Aelred's doctrine could be relevant is that of personal love between celibate men and women who are vowed to continence and chastity. The history of Christian monasticism contains many instances of such relationships; and there is no scarcity of men and women mystics who loved one another chastely, tenderly and radically. This is all the more remarkable when one reflects that the religious climate in which these holy celibates lived was geared to keep unmarried men and women segregated in all circumstances. Grilles and grates, enclosures and canonical censures were established to thwart any man-woman union outside marriage and to keep the sexes apart. But the mystics have always shown remarkable facility for beating the institution and transcending the cultural taboos of their day. They are the people who, with a smile and a song, really enjoy life; they are the people who lend energy to the thrust of life, dynamically leading the human family into the future. And so we find an Aelred-like friendship existing between St Teresa and St John of the Cross who were lifted up in a common ecstasy, she on one side of the convent grille and he on the other.

I do not vouch for the authenticity of the story I will now quote, though I myself have no objections to taking it literally. Even if spurious, it gives some indication of what pious hagiographers thought about friendship between the mystics:

It is related that on Trinity Sunday the two saints were conversing, separated by the convent grille, and that as St John held forth in burning language about the mystery which the Church celebrates that day, the heavens appeared to open, and their two souls, united in this sublime contemplation, soared upwards to the supreme Good, a glimpse of which had been vouchsafed to them. Whilst they were thus rapt in ecstasy, Sister Beatrice of Jesus, the portress, came to give a message to the prioress. She knocked; no one answered. She opened the door, and beheld the two saints lifted up into the air in ecstasy; St John holding on to the chair, vainly attempting to struggle with the force which impelled him upwards, St Teresa still on her knees, and also miraculously raised above the ground. News of the wondrous sight spread rapidly through the convent, and many came to witness it. The saint, interrogated afterwards by her daughters, answered: 'That is what comes of talking with Father John. Not only does he fall into an ecstasy, but he carries others away with him!'

(Lovat, p. 377)

What a sense of humour Teresa had – and how human! For the above (if it contains a germ of truth) was no more than a climactic moment in a close creative friendship of two extraordinary mystics, working together, freely exchanging ideas – while she darned his socks. This was a warm relationship – mystical and creative, yet totally celibate. Probably the great productivity of the two mystics had something to do with their mystical love and understanding. This is the opinion of a leading scholar in Carmelite studies who points out that neither could have reached their immense stature as spiritual writers without this friendship; and he believes that their incredible doctrinal achievement has its roots in their mutual cooperation and love.[1]

To the modern person, however, the puzzling feature of relationships like that of Teresa and John is their radical celibacy: the fact that both partners retained the highest ideals of chastity. A commingling of minds and hearts between two people separated by a lattice-work grille. Is this a Platonic rejection of the body?

While such relationships are rooted in a special charism that not everyone possesses, I do not believe that they contradict the laws of human psychology or that they put an intolerable strain on human nature. Nor are they Platonic. On this point I would like to quote

[1] See E. W. Trueman Dicken, *Ephemerides Carmeliticae*, vol. XXI (1970).

some observations of Viktor Frankl about a deep spiritual love that
exists (or, more correctly, can exist) at the core of man's being.
Physical sexuality, he maintains, is an expression of this love; but it
is not the only expression. And this love can grow and develop
without commingling of bodies. Here is what he says:

> Loving represents a coming to relationship with another as a
> spiritual being. The close connection with spiritual aspects of the
> partner is the ultimate attainable form of partnership. The lover
> is no longer aroused in his own physical being, nor stirred in his
> own emotionality, but moved to the depths of his spiritual core,
> moved by the partner's spiritual core. Love, then, is an entering
> into a direct relationship with the personality of the beloved . . .
> The lover's gaze looks through the physical and psychic dress to
> the spiritual core, looks to the core of the other's being. He is no
> longer interested in an alluring physical 'type' or attractive
> temperament; he is concerned with the person, with the partner
> as unique, irreplaceable and incomparable.   (Frankl, p. 108)

For Frankl, then, all true love is enacted at the deep core of the
being opened up through meditation (though not only through
meditation) and as such is a mystical experience. But he is not
precisely advocating celibacy, for he continues:

> All this, of course, is not to say that love has no desire to 'embody'
> itself. But it is independent of the body to the extent that it does
> not need the body. Even in love between the sexes the body, the
> sexual element, is not primary; it is not an end in itself, but a
> means of expression. Love as such can exist without it. Where
> sexuality is possible, love will desire and seek it; but where
> renunciation is called for, love will not necessarily cool or die . . .
> True love in and for itself needs the body neither for arousal nor
> for fulfilment, though it makes use of the body for both.
>   (Frankl, p. 112)

At our present stage of evolution the men and women who go
beyond the erotic and emotional to reach the spiritual core of another
are probably few in number. And perhaps only the mystics (or those
who aspire to mysticism) are capable of doing so. Yet the possibility
is there. And the mystics are the greatest friends. If they are a married

couple, they may express their love through sexual intercourse; if they are celibate, they practise restraint and renunciation. But in either case their love can be warm and growing and creative.

In this whole area, some of the richest and most challenging ideas flow from the pen of Teilhard de Chardin.[1] Radically dedicated to celibacy, he yet had the most intimate spiritual relationships with both men and women friends; and he experienced in the depth of his being the creativity that is unleashed by such encounters. As always, he sees friendship and spiritual love in their cosmic setting. Woman leads man out of his cramping isolation, pointing the way to a universal love that encompasses mankind and the whole universe, leading on to God. Moreover, man-woman love is the force that builds the cosmos and stimulates the thrust of life towards ever more fullness of being. Teilhard willingly admits that his most cherished ideas came to birth under feminine influence with its tender inspiration.

Casting his mind back millions of years, Teilhard sees the history of the universe as the development of an ever-evolving love. First, in inanimate matter, this love is no more than the interplay of molecular forces. With the birth of life and the growth of the biosphere, love is directed towards reproduction; but with the appearance of man, the reproductive function is accompanied by another dimension, a spiritual and personal dimension: now the couple build or create one another in a mutual complementarity. Indeed, as the human race evolves and develops, the reproductive function assumes a less important role. Matter is spiritualized; love is spiritualized; and in the course of time sexuality in the man will be satisfied by pure femininity.

In other words we have a human race evolving towards virginity which, far from being a denial of love, will be a magnificent expression of love of another kind. For Teilhard the greatness of woman is less in her physical maternity (important and beautiful though this is) than in her spiritual fecundity; and the man-woman relationship, particularly in its celibate form, unleashes the greatest energy in the

---

[1] See, for example, *Human Energy*, translated by J. M. Cohen (Collins, London, 1969, and Harcourt, Brace, Jovanovich, New York, 1970), pp. 32–4, 72–6, 128–30, 144–55; *The Evolution of Chastity; The Phenomenon of Man*, translated by Bernard Wall (Collins, London, and Harper, New York, 1959), pp. 264–8.

universe. This is the force that carries forward the thrust of life towards Omega, the personal centre of attraction, the ultimate point of convergence, the magnetic source of love from which nothing can separate us. In the final stage of unification in Omega, men will neither marry nor be given in marriage, 'but are like angels in heaven' (Mark 12:25).

Assuredly Teilhard's thought has its limitations.[1] Apart from the fact that it is written almost exclusively from the man's viewpoint, there is the additional fact that it just sounds fantastic. He himself admits this, saying that nine-tenths of mankind will consider him a naïve fool to entertain such outlandish ideas. But, he goes on, it is only because men attempted the impossible that we are able to fly and to travel in outer space. So why not attempt the impossible in human relations? Besides, few things are impossible if we have faith in man attracted by the ennobling call of Omega. Again, one might question his assumption that the man-woman relationship is the peak-point of evolution and the highest expression of human friendship. This is a claim which he does not adequately substantiate.

But an even greater limitation is the fact that in *The Evolution of Chastity* Teilhard asked the wrong question. Setting out to justify the celibate life, he presumed that virginity is superior to marriage and attempted to explain why this should be. As if the value of celibacy rested on its superiority to marriage. Surely it would have been better to place the two vocations side by side as parallel functions in the mystical body of Christ. This he could have done without jeopardizing his central insight; namely, that the celibates are men and women who feel the attraction of the divine centre drawing them to itself more acutely than the sexual attraction that might prematurely draw them together. This sense of vocation, which alone will justify celibacy (as it alone will explain marriage), is really the key to his thinking. But as often happens with pioneers, his conceptualization and articulation fall short of his intuition.

---

[1] Though Teilhard's thought has its limitations, he never compromises the traditional morality. I say this because it has been suggested that he was trying to justify sexual intercourse in a life dedicated to celibacy. This is nonsense and an utter travesty of his thought. He was trying to elaborate a theory of celibate love which, without being Platonic, would go beyond physical sex to the highest point in the spiritualization of matter.

If Teilhard is correct, mystical friendship will become a common phenomenon in the future. What was the exceptional privilege of a few will become the way of many. This is a remarkable prediction. If true, it proves again that the mystics are in the vanguard of evolution, challenging mankind to move forward to greater maturity and fullness of being. It points to the mystery and the richness and the wonder of one who loves 'the mountains, the solitary wooded valleys, strange islands . . . silent music'.

15. *Friendship – the cosmic dimension*

In the last chapter I referred to the Teilhardian observation that woman leads man out of his isolation. This she does by teaching him how to love. Through her he learns what it means to be loved and to love; and such an experience is ultimately 'ecstatic'. It carries him beyond the barriers of self into a wider world where he meets his truest love, who is 'the mountains, the solitary wooded valleys, strange islands . . . silent music'. Woman leads man to an enlightenment wherein he loses his little self to find his true self, the universe and God.

Probably all this is true of any love, not just that of man and woman. It is sometimes said that love is an exploration, a going out of self in quest of the mystery of the other; and in this search one goes endlessly on and on and on. For just as in the ascent of Mount Carmel one never comes face to face with God (the veil of faith is always there), so in the journey into the core of another, one never reaches the end. Mystery always remains – and, indeed, this very mystery is the enticing force that draws us on. Again, in the ascent of Mount Carmel one must never stop climbing; one must never be seduced by the beautiful flowers nor terrified by the wild beasts; one must leave all to find the treasure in an endless and anguishing purification. And in the same way, in the search for another one must never be seduced by secondary things: the peripheral joys, the sensual fascination, the ecstatic delights of intimacy. All this joy of friendship is good, exquisitely good; but one who clings to it refuses to grow.

The great enemy is absorption. Two people absorbed in one another are closed to the greater vibrations of the universe and the cosmic Christ. Settling down on a plateau, they will never scale the heights unless they break out of this closed circuit into the realm of cosmic creativity where they will build both the universe and one another. By renouncing absorption they find union which, while differentiating, renders one luminous to the other.

In true friendship, then, we find a movement away from absorption towards universality, away from self-centredness towards cosmification. Here is a strange combination of affection and detachment, of sincere personal love for another and limitless personal love for the universe, of deep emotional attachment without self-centred clinging. And just as in the ascent of Mount Carmel one sometimes gets ecstatic glimpses of the summit, so, in the journey into the dark being of another, one may get fleeting glimpses of that other's personal core. These glimpses are momentary and passing; they are cosmic experiences of God, because God is the centre of the other's being. If the mystics see the universe in a grain of sand, what must they see in the personal core of another?

All this is found in Aelred, at least in embryo. His third stage is a meeting with 'only Christ' – that is, with Christ inseparable from the universe and mankind and his Father. At the same time I believe that in this point Aelred's articulation, like that of Teilhard, falls short of his intuition. A cursory reading of his words might suggest that in the discovery of Christ (the kiss of 'only Christ') the human friend, so to speak, falls out of the picture and Christ alone remains. If Aelred meant this he would make friendship a *means* rather than a *way*. But I cannot think this was his intention. Rather did he mean that Christ is present as a third party towards whom the gaze of the friends is drawn while they remain closely united one to another – 'where two or three are gathered in my name, there am I' (Matthew 18:20). This is how Christ entered into the friendship of the two disciples going to Emmaus. He suddenly was present as a third person who had been walking with them all the time but only now appeared in visible form. The same is true of all the resurrection appearances of Christ: he is suddenly present as *another* in the midst of friends. Then their attention, no longer absorbed in one another, is drawn towards 'only Christ'. They are still united, closely united, but the pull of the divine centre is now so strong that it annihilates all tendency to absorption in one another, drawing their gaze towards itself. This was the situation of John and Teresa. Liberated from absorption in one another, they were united in a common gaze upon Christt.

And, of course, even this third stage is not the end of the friendship journey. The goal will only be reached with the *parousia*. This Aelred makes clear:

In this way, beginning with the love with which he has embraced

his friend, and rising up to the love with which he embraces
Christ, he will with great happiness enjoy the delight of the
friendship of friendships, awaiting the fullness of time . . . when
this friendship, to which in this life we admit only a few, will be
extended to all and by all will be extended to God, since God will
be All in all.   (Aelred, p. 702)

Here we find in Aelred an admirable combination of idealism and
realism. Idealism because his is a vision of friendship leading to
Omega and to an ultimate loving intimacy with all men. Yet he is
realistic enough to see that such a happy consummation can only
take place in 'the fullness of time'. After all, man at his present
evolutionary stage does not have the emotional wherewithal to be the
friend of everybody. What he can do, however, is *love* everybody – or
more correctly, anybody. And it is towards this universal love that
friendship moves when absorption has lost its grip.

The New Testament has good things to say about all this. First of
all there is the mysterious friendship of Jesus with his twelve disciples.
He has called them servants and then, at the end, he calls them friends.
Something like this transition from discipleship and subordination
to friendship and equality is found also in Buddhism. Once enlightened, the disciple is on a par with his master, because now he
has received all that the master has to give. And in some similar way,
in the last hours of his life, Jesus raises the status of these twelve
men from discipleship to friendship. At the last supper he says:

No longer do I call you servants, for the servant does not know
what his master is doing; but I have called you friends, for all that
I have heard from my Father I have made known to you.
                                                            (John 15:15)

No longer servants but friends, because he has opened his heart;
he has laid bare his soul; he has told them everything. And now there
is laid at their disposal what Paul vividly calls 'the unsearchable
riches of Christ' (Ephesians 3:8).
   What Jesus has revealed to them is not just a collection of parables
and teachings but his very self – for this is the word he has heard
from the Father. And the more they enter into the deepest self of
Christ, the more cosmic will they become. Because in the revelation

of himself Jesus reveals the Father – 'He who has seen me has seen the Father' (John 14:9). He also reveals the human race, which is his body; and he reveals the world, which was made by him even when it knew him not. That is why this friendship, which begins a few hours before his death, will never end.

In this whole matter we are strikingly confronted with the mysteriously cosmic dimension not only of Jesus but of any man. I once heard a Zen master, speaking to a group of Buddhists and Christians, say that the great enlightenment of Jesus was expressed in his word: 'Before Abraham was, I am' (John 8:58). This Zen master believed that here the 'I' of Jesus was not the little empirical ego, the illusory self that Buddhism rejects. Rather was it the 'I' of the universe that came surging up from the depth of his being in an ecstatic moment of awakening. While the master's faith obviously differed from mine, I felt that he was giving to Christians a new and valuable insight into the fact that the person of Christ is the eternal Word of the Father, cosmic and all-inclusive.

However this may be, the friendship of the disciples with their Lord became increasingly cosmic. The Church fathers loved to quote the words of Jesus: 'It is to your advantage that I go away' (John 16:7); and they would comment that by his departure and the ensuing separation Jesus was liberating the disciples from excess absorption, leading them on to the cosmic dimension of his risen existence. They might well have added that in all friendship separation plays an important role in leading friends away from absorption to an even greater universality.

The same evolutionary development is found in Paul. His letters show a growing intimacy with Christ, together with a growing thrust towards cosmification, reaching a climax in the later epistles where Paul enjoys the closest union with a risen Jesus who is co-extensive with the universe. Paul cannot adequately express his own experience (who could express such an experience?) but he speaks of the *secret* of Christ, hidden from all ages and only now made known (Colossians 1:26). There is a gradual revelation through the ages of a Christ who has been present in the heart of matter long before he is born as man in Israel. It is as though the incarnation of Christ is in some embryonic way contemporaneous with the birth of the universe. The Harvard astronomer Harlow Shapely put it well when he said, 'In the beginning was the word and the word was hydrogen gas.' He later protested that this remark was neither blasphemous nor facetious. What he meant was that the Word was somehow incarnate from the beginning in the very heart of matter. This, of course, is the Teilhardian approach to St Paul; and it fits in well with what we are saying here.

For as the Word was incarnate in hydrogen gas, so now in a more unique and personal way is it incarnate in the grand totality of the universe. This is the cosmic Christ, the secret now revealed and constantly being revealed as the universe moves toward the point of convergence where Omega stands triumphant. And Paul, who grasped the unsearchable riches of Christ, knew that friendship with him is friendship with the all.

It seems to me that Paul's friendship with Christ is a model or archetype of human friendships. These, too, have a cosmic dimension because (in the faith of the Christian and in the interpretation of Aelred) friendship with any man is ultimately friendship with Christ, just as to give a cup of water to anyone is to give a cup of water to Christ. This Christ who is the friend or to whom one gives the cup of water is cosmic, one with the Father and one with mankind. About the precise nature of this mysterious union of Christ with the all, however, little can be said; for this is an area that lies in the darkness of the cloud of unknowing. Here, perhaps, it is enough to recall once more the Teilhardian principle that union differentiates – to such an extent that the more a person becomes Christ the more he becomes himself. And that is why friendship with the other never excludes friendship with Christ, as friendship with Christ cannot exclude the other.

So the truest friendship leads to a universal love, a love of the cosmos and its mysterious source and of all men. Aelred comes to the love of God through the love of man: John of the Cross comes to the love of man through the love of God. Both end in the same place. In either case there is only one love, as is clear in the fourth gospel. 'That they may all be one; even as thou, Father, art in me, and I in thee, that they also may be in us, so that the world may believe . . .' (John 17:21). Christ and the Spirit and the Father and the human race are caught up in one mysterious but all-embracing love. There are not two loves, but only one.

And this love is the highest form of human energy. It is the life-force as well as the ultimate goal towards which the universe is straining and striving. As we look at the world today, the greatest problem is not air pollution, nor population explosion, nor sexual revolution, nor cultural change. The greatest problem is the imperfection of our love; that is to say, our lack of mysticism. And the people who carry forward the thrust of evolution are the mystics. They are the vanguard, ecstatically pointing towards the future.

EPILOGUE

16. *Convergence*

Almost fifty years ago, Alfred North Whitehead, commenting on the dwindling influence of Christianity and Buddhism, attributed their decline to a refusal to dialogue. 'The decay of Christianity and Buddhism as determinative influences in modern thought', he wrote, 'is partly due to the fact that each religion has unduly sheltered itself from the other. The self-sufficient pedantry of learning and the confidence of ignorant zealots have combined to shut up each religion in its own forms of thought. Instead of looking to each other for deeper meanings, they have remained self-satisfied and unfertilized. Both have suffered from the rise of the third tradition, which is science, because neither of them had retained the requisite flexibility of adaptation' (Whitehead, pp. 146, 140 ff.).

A good deal has happened since Whitehead penned these lines; and in the course of this book I have tried to say that Christianity and Buddhism are at last beginning to talk, to dialogue, to help one another: a process of cross-fertilization has now begun. Moreover, a Christian-Buddhist dialogue with science is under way, with scholars and researchers showing profound interest in the meditation and mysticism of Buddhist and Christian cultures. Where this three-cornered dialogue will end, no man can say. But it may well be a breakthrough in human history. It may be one of the most significant happenings of our day.

This is not the first experience of dialogue either for Christianity or for Buddhism. In the West a historic encounter took place when Christianity, basically a Jewish religion, met up with Hellenism and took into itself Greek thought-patterns and insights. This was an enrichment. And now, in the twentieth century, Christianity, conscious of its Jewish origins and maintaining its Hellenistic heritage, faces the indescribable wealth of the Eastern religions. How will she react? Where are we going? These are fascinating questions. For new vistas will now be opened; Western complacency will sustain new shocks; Western religion will be further liberated from age-old cultural and religious taboos. All in all, something new will be born.

In this book I have tried to stress what the great religions have in common. They share the same quest for wisdom, the same sense of man's existential situation and need of salvation, the same belief in man's dignity and value, the same basic attempt to solve man's deeper problems. I have also tried to say that science shares in the quest for wisdom; and in a rapidly converging world, where peoples and nations are coming together with unprecedented velocity, we need one another. We cannot survive unless we unite to build the earth and mould the human family into a single community. The world needs the Hindu experience of God gathered through many, many centuries of meditation and search. This is the experience of God immanent in nature, in the depth of being, at the core of the human soul. But, side by side with this, the world needs also the great Hebrew experience of the transcendent Yahweh who guides and loves while living beyond the reach of human thought or image. Again, the world needs the Buddhist unrelenting thirst for a wisdom which brings release and salvation through enlightenment. And the world cannot be deaf to the revelation of Jesus who, uniting in his person the transcendent and the immanent, speaks of God as no man ever spoke. And, finally, the world cannot survive without the scientist's untiring quest for truth, his work for human progress and for the betterment of man.

This is a far cry from saying that all these systems are the same. Far from being the same, they manifest a pluralism that is excitingly beautiful. They show us different ways, or *tao*, which lead to supreme wisdom. The word *tao* has fascinated me all through this book; and it is very relevant here. There are many paths to the summit of Mount Fuji, say the Japanese; and there are many religions that lead to something or someone who lies in impenetrable darkness beyond the cloud of unknowing. But unlike the paths of Fuji, the religions need one another. There are, moreover, many ways within each religious tradition. What a variety of ways exists in Mahayana Buddhism alone! And within Christianity, too, I have pointed to the ways of meditation, of purification and of friendship. But perhaps we could ask if there is anything common to all these ways. I believe there is.

In the Christian way the basic experience or enlightenment to which all the paths lead is that of being loved by God. This is the theme of the First Epistle of St John with its ever-recurring theme, 'We love, *because he first loved us*' (1 John 4:19). The author keeps reminding us that God took the initiative, that it was not my idea to love God, but rather that my love is the answer to a call or invitation. In other words, the first thing in Christianity is not my love for God and other people, but my belief that the world is loved by God. 'God is love'; and from this everything else follows. 'God so loved the world that he gave his only Son . . .' (John 3:16). From belief in God's love comes a sense of security, an unshakable faith that (in the words of Julian of Norwich) 'all will be well, and all will be well, and all manner of thing will be well'. It may look all wrong; but all will be well.

The basic enlightenment of the Old Testament has much in common with this. Here the stress is on the fidelity of God to his Covenant. God is faithful; he will not let you down; he will love in spite of everything. 'I have loved you with an everlasting love' (Jeremiah 31:3). And like a theme song through the pages of the Old Testament run the words, 'Fear not, for I am with you.' These are the words spoken to Moses and to Isaiah and to Jeremiah. The name is called (and how that name penetrates to the core of the being) and then the assurance given that all will be well. Things may be difficult; they may seem impossible; but I will be with you and nothing will harm you. And so again comes the sense of security, the great unshakable faith that 'all will be well, and all will be well, and all manner of thing will be well'.

In Hinduism, particularly in the *Gita*, we find the same stress on being loved, together with the joy and confidence released through such a conviction. Pure Land Buddhism, too, is based on the merciful love of Amida. Zen, it is true, does not speak in terms of being loved by God, since it says nothing about God at all. But enlightenment is accompanied by joy, a sense of security, the belief that 'all will be well, and all will be well, and all manner of thing will be well'.

In all these religions we have a common faith that is basically human. It is a faith in the future; it is faith like that of the mother who, clutching her child in her arms in the midst of earthquake, or flood or pestilence or war, tells him that all will be well. 'Fear not, for I am with you.' Viewed superficially, all is far from well; the situation may even call for despair; death may be imminent. But she has a true intuition that all will somehow be well. This is the intuition to which successful transactional analysis should lead: the belief that 'I'm OK and you're OK'. It is something that cannot be proved by reasoning and syllogism. In the last analysis I must make an act of faith. And the scientist, it seems to me, must have this faith too. He must have faith in man and in the future of the human race. Without such faith why make the effort? Why make the effort, unless I believe that thanks to this research 'all will be well, and all will be well, and all manner of thing will be well'?

This is the faith in man of which the poet spoke when he said that 'hope springs eternal in the human breast'. It is something common to the various ways. All must finally believe in man.

Perhaps we can also say that the great religions share a belief in a common destiny. It is as though one Spirit, filling and animating the universe, is driving us towards a point of convergence, a common point of intersection, where Buddhist and Christian, Hindu and Jew will meet. This point of convergence (call it Omega or what you will) may lie in the far, far distant future. We cannot see it; we cannot delineate it; but we are sure that it is there, even when we have no blueprint or construction model. I think that in interfaith dialogue we sometimes get a fleeting glimpse or foretaste of this ultimate union toward which we are tending – moments when Buddhists and Christians experience that they are one. Yet in this very dialogue, facing an uncertain future, we feel the need of guidelines to point out the way. During one dialogue which I myself attended a Japanese professor remarked good-humouredly that we all feel danger – cultural and religious danger to the values we cherish. He articulated the unexpressed sentiments of many. So let me tentatively suggest some guidelines.

First of all there is the fact that at our present stage of evolution we are on different, if intertwining, paths; and all the great religions wish to be faithful to their past and to their origins. We know that in the modern world fidelity to the past and to history is one of the great desires of individuals and of nations. There is no greater dread than that of losing one's religious and cultural heritage. Nor is this unreasonable. If (as psychoanalysis keeps reminding us) the individual is conditioned by his history, if the past is present within him, constantly pushing him on and influencing his conduct, the same is true of nations and of blocks of nations and of whole cultures. No man and no nation can deny the past without peril to psychological, cultural and religious life. That is why people must ordinarily remain in their own religious tradition unless conversion to another is the outgrowth of the past. The point of intersection and convergence has not yet arrived.

And to preserve the good things of the past, the great religions can be uncompromising without jeopardizing the harmony of dialogue. I myself feel this in regard to Christianity. If it is to be true to its New Testament roots, if it is to be honest in its dialogue with other religions, it has to be faithful to its founder – to the man, the carpenter, Jesus of Nazareth who, Christians believe, rose from the dead. To water down the divine Sonship of the historical Jesus with suggestions that we talk only about the *logos* or the cosmic Christ in the name of ecumenism is, it seems to me, unfair to the Buddhists, the Hindus, the Jews, the scientists with whom we dialogue. For Christianity is built on the belief that the *logos* 'emptied himself', became a very poor man, and lives now as the cosmic Christ. This is the peculiar contribution which Christianity makes to the world; and without it, what would Christianity have to offer?

The first guideline, then, is fidelity to the past. But this alone is not enough. The great religions must also march into the future in accordance with the inexorable law of progress, of change, of evolution. Paradoxical though it sounds, in order to be faithful to the past we must be detached from this very past to face the future with a readiness to change. Only in this way can we make progress along the path which leads to Omega.

Finally, it should be remembered that the evolutionary process is not automatic. It must be carried forward by men and women in an ongoing dialogue with one another and with the world. This book has been written in the belief that meditation is a key factor in this dialogue and in the march forward of humanity. For the meditator or the mystic, going beyond thoughts and concepts and images to a deeper level of awareness, finds himself in an ever growing union with the universe and with others – a union which is enacted at the core of his being. And when he enters into dialogue with others who also are meditators or mystics, both may find themselves in a remarkable harmony, even when their conceptual systems and symbols differ radically. They may find that they are dwelling in one another, sharing a common vision as they move towards a common future. This vision cannot be conceptualized. It is certain with the certainty of faith; but it is also obscure because of this very faith.

But the mystic is more particularly the builder of the future because he loves. Throughout this book I have insisted that in the last analysis meditation is a love affair and that love is the most powerful energy in the universe. It is love that builds the earth and carries forward the thrust of evolution. It is love that brings together the great traditions in a union which cross-fertilizes even when it differentiates. It is love that leads them on towards Omega, the point of convergence, which is also 'the mountains, the solitary wooded valleys, strange islands . . . silent music'.

Glossary of words used in the text

agape (Greek), love: used in the New Testament to designate the special reality of Christian love, whose source is the Spirit. It refers in the first place to God's love for men, but also to the love of Christians for one another and for God.

anatta (Pali), *muga* (Japanese), non-self: *anatta doctrine* is the Buddhist teaching that there is no permanent self.

bodhisattva (Sanskrit): in Buddhism, an enlightened person dedicated to helping others reach liberation. He represents the last stage before that of supremely enlightened, fully perfected Buddhahood.

chakras (Sanskrit): centres of energy in the human body. In Hindu tradition there are seven such centres, located, (1) at the base of the spine; (2) at the base of the male genital organ; (3) in the lumbar region; (4) in the cardiac region; (5) in the laryngeal region; (6) between the eyebrows; (7) at the top of the head. In Tantric Buddhism there are only four centres, situated in the umbilical, cardiac, laryngeal regions, and the cerebral plexus.

dokusan (Japanese): in Zen Buddhism, a private interview with the *roshi* for spiritual direction.

eschaton (Greek), the last day: in biblical theology *eschaton* refers to the consummation of history when the risen Christ will return for judgement.

guru (Sanskrit), teacher, venerable one: in Eastern tradition, a *guru* is a religious master or a spiritual director.

Hesychasm: a method of prayer in the Oriental Christian Church that depended on control of the physical faculties, and concentration on the *Jesus Prayer* to achieve peace of soul and union with God. Originally a monastic practice, it was popularized in the thirteenth and fourteenth centuries.

imprimatur (Latin), literally, 'let it be printed': in the Roman Catholic Church, this word was the official sign of permission for a book to be printed. It was, therefore, the mark of orthodoxy in Catholic books prior to the Second Vatican Council (1962–65).

jiriki (Japanese), self-reliance.

kairos (Greek), time, the right season. In Greek philosophy *kairos* was used to designate a critical period or moment of decision. The *kairos* in Scripture is the time of salvation which God has chosen and decreed to offer the fullness of grace in Jesus Christ. It is therefore also the critical moment in which the final judgement begins.

Kannon (Japanese), also *Kwannon*, and in Sanskrit, *Avalokiteshvara: Kannon*, meaning 'the great compassionate one', is the Buddhist saint (*bodhisattva*) of universal love who plays a central role in the devotional practices of all Buddhist sects.

koan (Japanese), paradoxical problem pointing to ultimate truth. It is meaningless to the rational intellect and can only be solved by awakening a deeper level of the mind, beyond discursive thought.

kyrios (Greek), lord or ruler. *Kyrios* was used in the Septuagint as a translation of the divine name, *Yahweh*. In New Testament times, the Early Church used it as a title of praise and adoration for the risen Jesus. By calling the risen Jesus, *Kyrios* (the Lord), the Church acknowledged him to be God.

Logos (Greek), word. *Logos* is the title given in John 1: 1–14 and 1 John 1 to Jesus as the Son of God. The Latin translated it as *Verbum* and in English it is 'the Word'. In biblical theology *Logos* is used for Jesus Christ, the Word made flesh.

makyo (Japanese), *maya* (Sanskrit), illusion or ignorance of the true nature of things. Specifically, *makyo* sometimes refers to the hallucinatory phenomena one may experience at a certain period in the practice of *zazen*.

mandala (Sanskrit), circle, assemblage or picture. In Tantric Buddhism, the *mandala* is a sacred symbol full of cosmic significance.

mantra (Sanskrit), prayer or hymn. The *mantra* in Tantric Buddhism and in other Eastern traditions is a sacred word given by the master to the disciple at the time of initiation. When the disciple's mind is properly attuned, the inner vibrations of this word-symbol, together with its associations in his mind, are said to lead to mind-expansion. One such sacred word is 'Om'.

miccha samadhi (Pali), *mithya samadhi* (Sanskrit), a state of one-pointedness (*samadhi*) about the wrong thing. It is roughly equivalent to false mysticism.

nirvana (Sanskrit), literally, extinction (of individual existence); from *nirva*, to be extinguished or blown out. In Buddhism, *nirvana* is the highest mystical experience of changelessness, inner peace and freedom, attained through the extinction of the self. It denotes a return to the Buddha nature after the dissolution of the physical body; a state of perfect bliss and freedom, beyond life and death.

noosphere, literally, the realm of the mind (Greek, *nous*). Teilhard de Chardin used *noosphere* in a particular way to designate the realm or sphere which encloses human thought and love. He likened it to the biosphere in which all living things are in contact and interaction with each other. The *noosphere* is superimposed on the biosphere, and comprises all psychosocial and cultural changes, all artistic and scientific achievements, in short, all human achievements and values.

Omega (Greek): *Omega* is the last letter in the Greek alphabet. Teilhard de Chardin used this word in two particular contexts: (1) to signify the end point or term of the natural evolution of mankind and the cosmos; the apex of the convergent social and spiritual development on earth; (2) for God, as a pre-existent, transcendent and immanent superperson who is the loving and lovable and omnipresent activating centre, source and goal of noogenesis. For Teilhard, *Omega* was the risen Christ as depicted by St Paul and St John.

parousia (Greek): In biblical theology, a term used to designate Christ's second coming at the end of history. Its approximate meaning is 'saving presence' or 'arrival'.

pleroma (Greek), literally, that which fills up; a fullness or completeness. In biblical theology, the *pleroma* is the fullness of divine excellence and powers which will be complete at the *parousia*.

prajna (Sanskrit), supreme knowledge or wisdom.

Rinzai (Japanese): one of the two prominent Zen sects in Japan. The other is *Soto*.

roshi (Japanese), Zen master.

samadhi (Sanskrit), *san'mai* (Japanese): in a broad sense *samadhi* refers to a state of heightened and expanded awareness beyond conceptual thought. In this book it is used in this sense, to denote an intense yet effortless concentration, reaching a state of one-pointedness, peace and equilibrium.

samurai (Japanese), a warrior: the *samurai* were the military aristocracy of feudal Japan. *Samurai* also refers to the individual knights or warriors of this social caste. They had the power of life and death over commoners. Their special privileges were abolished with the fall of feudalism in 1871.

sapientia (Latin), wisdom.

satori (Japanese), the experience of enlightenment, i.e., self-realization, opening the mind's eye, awakening to one's true nature and hence to the nature of existence.

sesshin (Japanese): in Zen Buddhism, *sesshin* is a kind of monastic retreat (usually of seven days) devoted principally to long periods of *zazen* in a concentrated and intense effort to achieve enlightenment.

siddhis (Sanskrit), literally, perfections: in Eastern meditation *siddhis* are parapsychological powers (for example, clairvoyance or telepathy) which one may acquire at a certain stage of meditation.

silentium mysticum (Latin), mystical silence. This term is used in Christian mystical theology to denote a state of quiet beyond conceptual thought in which the spirit rests in a sense of God's presence.

Soto (Japanese): one of the two prominent sects of Zen Buddhism in Japan. The other is *Rinzai*.

sutra (Sanskrit): the Buddhist scriptures containing dialogues and sermons attributed to the Buddha.

swami (Hindu), *svamin* (Sanskrit), lord, master, king. In Hindu tradition, *swami* is a title (like 'Reverend') given to a religious teacher.

tao (Chinese), literally, a road, a way; figuratively, the course of nature, the absolute, the cosmic order. Thus it means also truth, or right conduct.

zazen (Japanese), sitting in Zen meditation.

Books and articles quoted in the text

Aelredi, Beati, Abbatis Rievallensis: *Opera Omnia* (Editio Migne, Paris, 1855).

Burtt, E. A. (editor): *The Teachings of the Compassionate Buddha* (The New American Library, New York, 1955).

Chang, Garma: *The Practice of Zen* (Harper & Row, New York, 1970).

Francis de Sales, St: *Introduction to the Devout Life*, translated and edited by John K. Ryan (Harper Brothers, New York, 1949).

Frankl, Viktor E.: *The Doctor and the Soul* (Alfred A. Knopf, New York, 1955).

Green, Elmer (1): 'Conference on Voluntary Control of Internal States', in *Psychologia* 12: 107–8 (1969).

Green, Elmer (2): *Psychophysiological Training for Creativity* (Research Department, The Menninger Foundation, Topeka, Kansas, 1971).

Green, Elmer (3): 'Voluntary Control of Internal States: Psychological and Physiological', in *Journal of Transpersonal Psychology*, vol. 11, no. 1 (1970).

Green, Elmer (4): 'On the Meaning of Transpersonal', in *Journal of Transpersonal Psychology*, vol. 3, no. 1 (1971).

Green, Elmer (5): *Biofeedback for Mind-Body Self-Regulation* (Research Department, The Menninger Foundation, Topeka, Kansas, 1971).

Green, Elmer (6): *Preliminary Report on Voluntary Control Project: Swami Rama* (The Menninger Foundation, Topeka, Kansas, 1970).

Guibert, Joseph de: *The Theology of the Spiritual Life* (Sheed & Ward, New York and London, 1953 and 1954).

Hirai, Tomio: *The Psychophysiology of Zen* (Igaku Shoin, Tokyo, 1974).

Ignatius of Loyola, St: *The Spiritual Exercises of St Ignatius*, translated by Anthony Mottola, introduction by Robert Gleason, SJ (Doubleday, New York, 1963).

John of the Cross, St: *The Collected Works of St John of the Cross*, translated by Kieran Kavanaugh, OCD, and Otilio Rodriguez, OCD (Institute of Carmelite Studies, Washington, DC, 1973).

Johnston, William (editor) (1): *The Cloud of Unknowing and the Book of Privy Counselling* (Doubleday, New York, 1973).

Johnston, William (2): *The Still Point* (Harper & Row Perennial Library, New York, 1971).

Lovat, Lady Alice: *The Life of St Teresa* (Herbert & Daniel, London, 1911).

Naranjo, Claudio, and Ornstein, Robert: *On the Psychology of Meditation* (Viking Press, New York, 1971).

Poulain, Auguste: *Des Grâces d'Oraison* (Paris, 1901).

Segal, Julius (editor): *Mental Health Program Reports – 5* (National Institute of Mental Health, Rockville, Md., 1971).

Tart, Charles (editor): *Altered States of Consciousness* (John Wiley, New York, 1969).

Teresa of Avila, St (1): *The Life of Saint Teresa of Avila* by herself, translated by J. M. Cohen (Penguin Books, Harmondsworth and Baltimore, Md., 1957).

Teresa of Avila, St (2): *The Interior Castle*, translated by E. Allison Peers (Doubleday, New York, 1961).

Teresa of Avila, St (3): *The Way of Perfection*, translated by E. Allison Peers (Doubleday, New York, 1964).

Wapnick, Kenneth: 'Mysticism and Schizophrenia', in *Journal of Transpersonal Psychology*, vol. 1, no. 2 (1969).

Weide, Thomas: 'Council Grove IV – Toward a Science Concerned with Ultimates', in *Journal of Transpersonal Psychology*, vol. 6, no. 1 (1972).

Whitehead, Alfred N.: *Religion in the Making* (Cambridge University Press, Cambridge, 1926, and World Publishing Company, New York, 1954). (Page references are given for both editions.)

Index